How to Study Your Bible

by Thomas D. Lea

With practical learning exercises by BILL LATHAM
Leader's Guide by Don Atkinson

Convention Press
Nashville, Tennessee

© Copyright 1986, 1998 • Convention Press
7th reprint 1999
All rights reserved

ISBN 0-7673-1915-X

This book is the text for the course CG-0102 in the subject area
Bible Studies in the Christian Growth Study Plan

Dewey Decimal Classification: 248.4
Subject Heading: CHRISTIAN LIFE\SALVATION

Unless stated otherwise, the Scripture quotations in this book are from the
NEW AMERICAN STANDARD BIBLE. © Copyright The Lockman Foundation,
1960, 1962, 1963, 1968, 1971, 1972, 1973, 1975, 1977. Used by permission.

Excerpt from *Master Study Bible*, New American Standard Version,
pages 58-59, used by permission of The Lockman Foundation,
© 1960, 1962, 1963, 1968, 1971, 1972, 1973, 1975, 1977.

Order additional copies of this book by writing to Customer Service Center,
MSN 113; 127 Ninth Avenue, North; Nashville, TN 37234-0113;
by calling toll free (800) 458-2772; by faxing (615) 251-5933;
by ordering online at *www.lifeway.com*; by emailing *customerservice@lifeway.com*;
or by visiting a LifeWay Christian Store.

For information about adult discipleship and family resources, training, and events,
visit our Web site at *www.lifeway.com/discipleplus*.

Printed in the United States of America

Discipleship and Family Adult Department
LifeWay Christian Resources
127 Ninth Avenue, North
Nashville, Tennessee 37234

*As God works through us,
we will help people and churches know Jesus Christ and seek His kingdom
by providing biblical solutions that spiritually transform individuals and cultures.*

Contents

How to Use This Book   7
Introduction   8
One Prerequisite for Bible Study   12
Two Rules to Guide Bible Study   22
Three Ways to Do Bible Study   42
Four Areas to Apply Bible Study   76
Five Aids to Understanding Bible Study   96
Conclusion   127
Leader's Guide   128
Christian Growth Study Plan   144

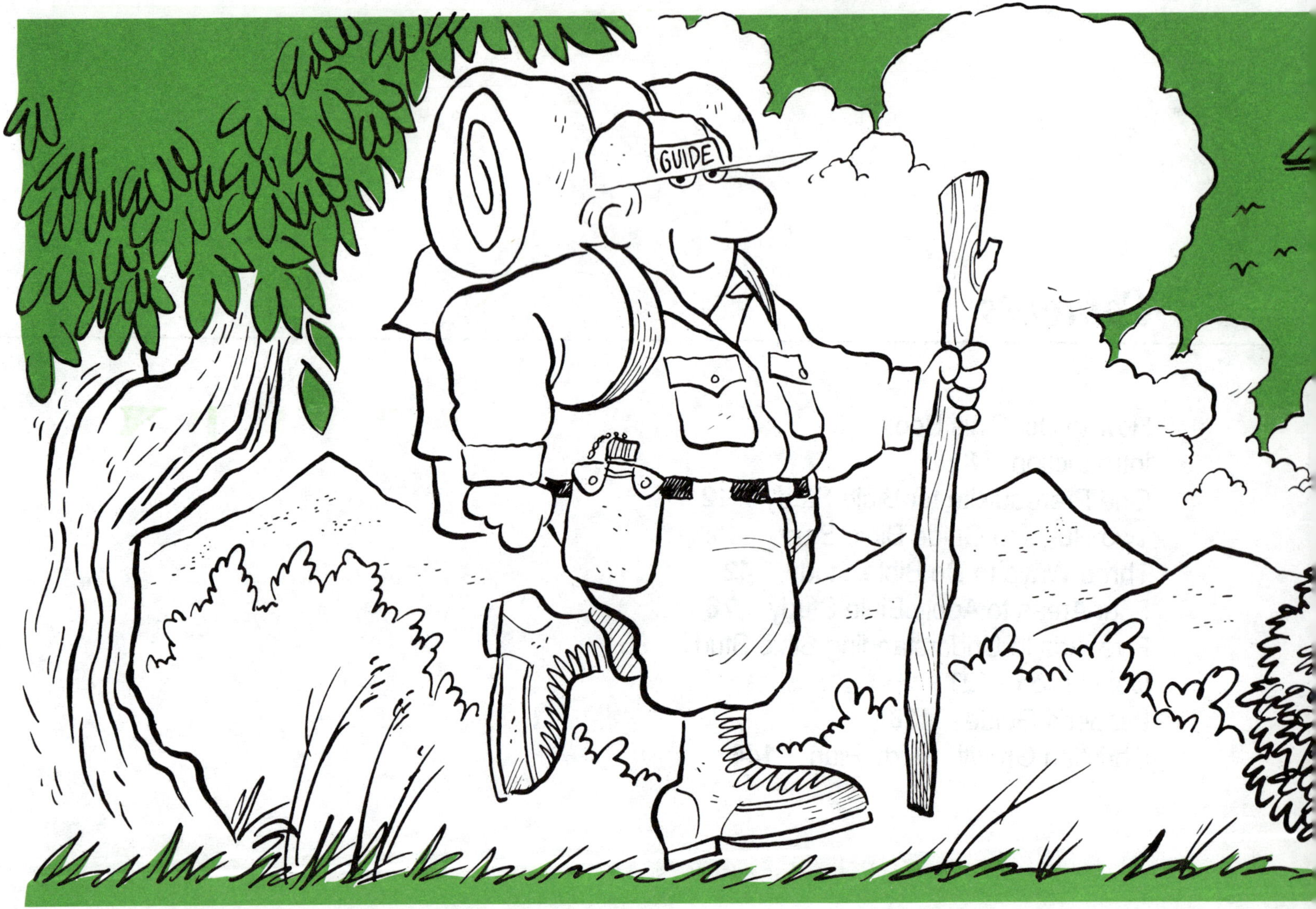
GUIDE

How to Use This Book

1. Read the introductory pages.
2. Remove the Scripture memory verses from the center, cut them out, and begin to memorize two of them each week.
3. Set apart a definite time and place to study your Bible. Use the material in this book to guide those times.
4. Do not do more than one day's work at a time. **Do** be consistent in your daily study time, doing five days of study in this book each week.

Beginning to Study Your Bible

The law of the Lord is perfect, restoring the soul;
The testimony of the Lord is sure, making wise the simple;
The precepts of the Lord are right, rejoicing the heart;
The commandment of the Lord is pure, enlightening the eyes.
(Ps. 19:7-8)

The psalmist is telling us of the importance of Scripture in our lives. God can use Scripture to revive us, give us wisdom, provide us joy, and open our eyes spiritually.

Our problem is that all too few Christians are involved in hearing, reading, studying, and learning the Scriptures. That is the problem which we are trying to overcome in presenting *How to Study Your Bible*.

How to Study Your Bible will major on teaching *how* to study the Bible. We will approach the Bible with several different methods of study. Using these methods can provide a many-sided view of the contents of the Bible. We will learn how to approach an entire book of the Bible or a brief passage. We will learn how to study a Bible character or a trait of character. We will learn about investigating the history, geography, and culture in the Bible. We also will learn about understanding the theology of a passage. We will major on the application of a passage in our own lives.

In addition to learning about studying the Bible, Scripture memory will be emphasized. Twenty-two Scripture memory cards appear in this guide. You can memorize these verses at the rate of two a week as you work through the lessons of the book. Memorizing will add to your own understanding of the teachings of Scripture. As you memorize the Scripture, you also can meditate on what you have memorized. This act of meditation can increase your grasp of the teaching of the passage and its application.

We have laid out the contents of *How to Study Your Bible* using the fingers of a hand. Look at the figure and try to understand how this study is organized.

Hand diagram:
1. PREREQUISITE FOR BIBLE STUDY
2. RULES TO GUIDE BIBLE STUDY
3. WAYS TO DO BIBLE STUDY
4. AREAS TO APPLY BIBLE STUDY
5. AIDS TO UNDERSTANDING BIBLE STUDY

First, we will learn the prerequisite for Bible study. The first week of lessons will emphasize that a child of God must be spiritually hungry in order to study and understand the Bible. One who studies the Bible must be eager to learn, teachable in spirit, and thoroughly dependent on the Holy Spirit for understanding. There also must be discipline. Studying the Bible is thrilling and exciting, but it does require effort and hard work.

Second, we will learn two rules to guide Bible study. We will study these during the second and third weeks. In the second week we will learn guidelines for interpreting what the Bible says. In the third week we will learn principles for applying the message of the Bible in life. These studies can give us more accuracy and insight as we study the Bible.

Third, we will learn three ways to do Bible study. This will be our study during weeks 4-6. In the fourth week we will learn how to approach a complete book of the Bible. We will learn to get an overview of what the book is teaching. We also will learn how to outline the book. In the fifth week we will learn how to study a brief passage of Scripture. We will seek to understand its content and apply it in our lives. In the sixth week our study will include the history, geography, and culture of the Bible. Learning these background facts can cause the Bible to become lively and understandable when otherwise it might be puzzling.

Fourth, we will learn four areas to apply Bible study. This study will occupy weeks 7 and 8. The Bible has a message which we can use in our own lives and which we can share with others. The Bible teaches us about God and tells us what God expects of His people, the church. We will use the study of the characters of the Bible and devotional study of the Bible in order to apply the Bible to all of these areas.

Fifth, we will learn five aids to understanding Bible study. This study will come during weeks 9-11. These studies will not always be different methods of Bible study. They will include some principles which can improve our study habits in all our work with the Bible. We will learn how to understand the words and figures of speech which appear in the Bible. We will study the grammar of the Bible in order to improve our understanding of what God is saying. Our study of the topics of the Bible will give us an organized picture of what the Bible teaches on many subjects. We also will learn to use the Bible to understand the doctrine of Scripture.

The hand diagram will serve as a reminder of what each section contains. Remember, we will approach the Bible with:
1 *Prerequisite for Bible Study*. We must be spiritually hungry children of God.
2 *Rules to Guide Bible Study*. We must understand how to interpret the Bible and how to apply its message.
3 *Ways to Do Bible Study*. We must understand the overview of a book, the details of a passage, and the background of the passage.
4 *Areas to Apply Bible Study*. We will apply the Bible in our understanding of God and ourselves, others, and our church.
5 *Aids to Understanding Bible Study*. We will learn to understand the words, figures of speech, grammar, topics, and doctrines of the Bible.

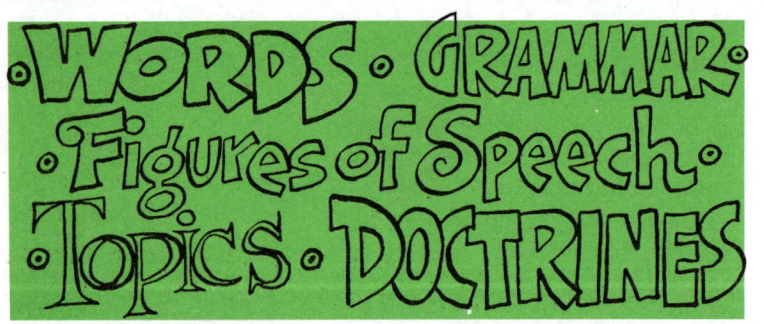

Using How to Study Your Bible

As you approach each part of your journey through Bible study, you will have five daily assignments for eleven weeks. Each daily assignment contains a discussion of the principle or fact about Bible study which you need to understand. Scattered throughout the assignment are exercises which you should complete. Finishing these exercises will assure that you have understood what the lesson is teaching. Neglecting them will mean that you come through each lesson with only a partial understanding.

Most of the lessons will involve between twenty and thirty minutes of daily time. Some lessons will be longer or shorter than others. As you follow each lesson, you may discover a special interest which will lead you to spend some additional time. This is up to you. Just be sure to finish the basic lesson.

Twice a week you will find a reference to a Scripture verse(s) which you will need to memorize. A group of Scripture memory cards is attached to the middle section of the study. Remove these cards and use scissors to cut apart the verses for each day. Memorize the verses which apply to your assignment for the week.

No topics have been given for the verses. You may wish to give your own topics and learn them as a part of the verses.

You will face many temptations for the use of your time as you begin *How to Study Your Bible*. Determine from the start to let nothing prevent you from progressing toward your goal. Remember, your goal is to improve your knowledge and understanding of the Bible.

Some Books You Will Need

In many of the daily lessons I will refer to some Bible study helps which you can use to assist your study. I am listing some helps which you can find in many church media libraries. If you don't find these specific books, substitutes will be in most libraries.

1. COMMENTARY: *The Broadman Bible Commentary,* ed. Clifton J. Allen. Nashville: Broadman Press, 1969.
2. BIBLE SURVEY: Old Testament, *Introduction to the Old Testament* by Roland K. Harrison. Grand Rapids: Eerdmans, 1969. New Testament, *Survey of the New Testament* by Robert H. Gundry. Grand Rapids: Zondervan, 1982.
3. BIBLE HISTORY: Old Testament, *Israel and the Nations* by F. F. Bruce. Grand Rapids: Eerdmans, 1963.
   New Testament, *The New Testament World* by H. E. Dana. Nashville: Broadman, 1937.
4. BIBLE CULTURE: *Biblical Backgrounds* by J. McKee Adams. Nashville: Broadman, 1965.
5. CONCORDANCE: *Analytical Concordance to the Bible* by Robert Young. New York: Funk and Wagnalls, n.d.
6. TOPICAL BIBLE: *Nave's Topical Bible* by Orville J. Nave. Chicago: Moody, n.d.
7. WORD STUDIES: *An Expository Dictionary of New Testament Words* by W. E. Vine. Westwood, N.J.: Revell, 1940.
8. BIBLE ATLAS: *Baker's Bible Atlas* by Charles F. Pfeiffer. Grand Rapids: Baker Book House, 1961.
9. BIBLE DICTIONARY: *The New Bible Dictionary,* ed. J. D. Douglas. Grand Rapids: Eerdmans, 1962.
10. BIBLE ENCYCLOPEDIA: *The Zondervan Pictorial Encyclopedia of the Bible,* ed. Merrill C. Tenney. Grand Rapids: Zondervan, 1975.

WEEK 1, DAY 1

THIS UNIT: *One Prerequisite for Bible Study*
TODAY: *Being a Child of God*

Read 1 Corinthians 2:14.

Welcome to *How to Study Your Bible!* Perhaps this is your first time to work with any of the Survival Kit materials; or you may be a veteran who already has completed all the other studies in the Survival Kit series. Whichever the case may be, you can look forward to eleven weeks of study that will give new life and deeper meaning to your personal Bible study.

Whether you are a newcomer or a veteran, you need the information in the introduction. Take time to read those pages now if you have not already done so.

In the introduction you learned that you would study in five different areas. What is the area in which you begin?

1 P _ _ _ _ _ _ _ _ _ _ _ _

You learned that **ONE PREREQUISITE** is necessary for Bible study, and you learned what that prerequisite is. Write it here.

A S _ _ _ _ _ _ _ _   H _ _ _ _ _

If your Bible study is to be effective, you must have a spiritual hunger for God's Word. That's what you will be studying about this week—developing and maintaining a true hunger to know more about God's Word. Today you will study about one important prerequisite to hungering for God's Word. What do you think that prerequisite might be? What is the first and most important condition you think you had to meet before you could begin to hunger for and understand the truths of God's Word? Write your answer to that question here.

_____

You are exactly right if you said that it was necessary for you to become a Christian or a child of God first.

It is surprising, isn't it, how some people think they become God's children. Take time now to read the comment in the illustration. What would you reply? Write your reply in the illustration.

WHAT WOULD YOU SAY?

I'VE BEEN KIND TO PEOPLE ALL MY LIFE. I'VE BEEN A GOOD FATHER AND HUSBAND. I GO TO CHURCH WHEN I CAN. SURELY GOD WILL LET ME INTO HEAVEN.

Does this sound familiar? Have you ever thought this? Perhaps you have heard others say this. What is the speaker relying on as his hope for heaven? Christ or his own efforts? If you said his own efforts, you are on target.

What does the Bible teach as the right hope for heaven? Notice what Paul says in Titus 3:5: "He saved us, not on the basis of deeds which we have done . . . but according to His mercy." Our hope is in God's mercy which He showed in Jesus Christ. We can't earn a trip to heaven by our own efforts.

It is hard for a person who is not a child of God to admit that his own works won't earn heaven for him. When we realize that we are sinners, we also realize that our deeds will never be good enough to earn heaven.

How do we join God's family? We become a child of God by faith in Jesus Christ. "As many as received Him, to them He gave the right to become children of God" (John 1:12).

Eternal life is a gift of God through faith in Jesus Christ. Eternal life does not come from our own efforts. A child of God, a Christian, knows this. Often an outsider, a non-Christian, does not understand it. The teachings of the Bible are best understood by those who are children of God.

Paul expressed this truth in 1 Corinthians 2:14: "A natural man does not accept the things of the Spirit of God; for they are foolishness to him." The word *natural* refers to a man who does not have the Holy Spirit. He is not a Christian. To this person the teachings of Scripture often don't make sense. The commands and promises of the Bible may be puzzling and unrealistic to one who is not a child of God.

Jesus talked to Nicodemus about the same idea. He said that Nicodemus needed to be "born again" in order to see the kingdom of God (John 3:3). Nicodemus' statements and questions show that he lacked the ability to grasp what Jesus was saying. A non-Christian cannot fully grasp the spiritual truths which are taught from the Bible. The apostle John said: "We are from God; he who knows God listens to us; he who is not from God does not listen to us" (1 John 4:6).

Why is the Bible clear only to a child of God? One reason is that a Christian has the Holy Spirit. The Holy Spirit is the teacher of God's truths (John 14:26). He makes God's commands and promises easier to understand. Another reason is that the Christian has had experiences that help in understanding the Bible. Family members sometimes will laugh or chuckle when certain words are mentioned. If I am an outsider, I won't understand what is funny. I am not a family member and have not experienced the humor of that word.

The Bible is a message to members of God's family. The family can understand the Bible because the family members have the experience to grasp it.

Do you want to study the Bible? Do you want to understand what you study? Do you want your life to be changed by what you read? Yes, you do! But you must be a child of God in order to understand and apply the Bible to your life.

Memorizing Scripture will be one of the most important elements in your study, and you will begin memorizing in this first session. You *can* memorize. Perhaps you haven't tried to memorize since you were in school, but you can still do it. The key is to have a positive attitude, work at it each day, and review regularly. The Scripture memory cards at the center of your book will help you. If you haven't already cut these apart, do so now. The Scripture you read at the beginning of this session is your first memory assignment. Use the appropriate Scripture memory card and begin memorizing 1 Corinthians 2:14.

WEEK 1, DAY 2

THIS UNIT: *One Prerequisite for Bible Study*
TODAY: *Eagerness to Learn About God*

Read Psalm 1.

Do you want to understand and apply the Bible to your life? You must be a spiritually hungry child of God. The Bible will make sense only if you are this kind of person.

Yesterday you learned that only a child of God can truly understand the Bible. Today you will find that understanding the Bible demands an eagerness to learn about God.

Which one of the following is more eager to buy a new car:
- The detailed discusser who talks at home with a reluctant wife or husband about the need for a new car?
- The glass gazer who stares through showroom windows at the various colors and models of new cars?
- The purposeful purchaser who discusses, gazes, and compares before deciding on a specific car at a certain cost to meet a definite need?

The purposeful purchaser is eager to buy the car. The detailed discusser might back away if he meets family opposition. The glass gazer might be curious and not committed. The sticker shopper will leave a car in the showroom if the price is too high.

There are at least three different types of Bible students. Let's look at these three to see what you can learn that will help you with your own personal Bible study. The first type of Bible student is the one who studies the Bible, but not because of a spiritual hunger for God's truths. I guess we could say that these people study the Word of God for secondary reasons. These reasons certainly are not the most important reason. Make a list of what you think are secondary reasons that people study God's Word.

SOME PEOPLE STUDY THE BIBLE, BUT FOR ALL THE WRONG REASONS.

Did you list curiosity about religion and about Bible facts? You could have listed loyalty to a Bible study group or to a teacher. Look at your list again. Add to it any other ideas you have. Then put a check beside secondary motives that you have been aware of in your own life at some time.

The second type of Bible student is the would-be student. He lets circumstances keep him from Bible study. The circumstances may include personal pleasure such as watching television or attending sports events. Job activity can make a person too tired to want to spend time in Bible study. Sickness or accidents can weaken a person so that he gets off the track of Bible study.

Sometimes people may interfere with the Bible study of other people. For example, some Christians have studied the Bible during a lunch break. Then they have quit when other workers called them too religious. A college roommate may complain about a desk light which is shining too late or too early. The Christian roommate may "sleep in" rather than study the Bible.

List in the illustration some of the distractions that keep persons from being serious students of the Bible.

> **SOME PEOPLE HAVE ALL THE GOOD INTENTIONS IN THE WORLD, BUT THEY STILL DO NOT STUDY THE BIBLE.**
> _____
> _____
> _____
> _____

If you are like me, you did not have any trouble completing that list. I suppose we all have trouble with distractions. Look at your list again and check the distractions that cause you the greatest difficulty.

The person who will learn and apply the teachings of the Bible is one whose eagerness will overcome all obstacles. Psalm 1:2 pronounces the blessings of God on a person whose "delight is in the law of the Lord" and who meditates on that law "day and night." These words describe a person who is eager to know and obey God. The psalmist is picturing a person who conducts his life and business during the day by the principles of the Bible. He measures his actions at the end of the day by God's standards in the Bible.

Notice the words of the psalmist in Psalm 19:7-14. Here the psalmist shows a high regard for God's message by describing it with words such as "perfect," "sure," "pure," and "clean." He is eager to learn the Bible because it warns him of pitfalls to avoid. It also promises him great rewards. He loves the Bible because it offers him inner cleansing. He is eager to study the Bible because it offers him victory over deceitful, enslaving sins.

Observe the devotion of the psalmist in Psalm 119:9-11. He wants cleansing, purity, and preservation from sin. He presents himself before God with obedience, commitment, and purity. He is eager to learn about God.

I hope that I can help your motivation to grow to the extent that you become a genuinely eager student of the Word. Stop now and think. What needs do you have, and what benefits do you hope to receive that make you want to be a better student of God's Word? List them in the illustration.

> **THERE ARE LOTS OF REASONS TO BE EAGER TO STUDY GOD'S WORD.**
> _____
> _____
> _____
> _____

End your study time today with a special time of prayer. Examine again the three lists you have made during this session. Then pray asking God to help you to develop a genuine eagerness to study His Word and ask Him to help you to deal with the distractions that would keep you from your study.

WEEK 1, DAY 3

THIS UNIT: One Prerequisite for Bible Study
TODAY: A Teachable Attitude

Your Reading Assignment Will Come Later.

Keep in mind that you are studying about **ONE PREREQUISITE** that you must have if you are to be a student of God's Word. That prerequisite is a spiritual hunger to know God's Word. So far you have learned that having that spiritual hunger requires that you be a child of God and that you have an eagerness to learn. Today you will see that you also must have a teachable attitude.

Your reading assignment today is Psalm 119. This psalm uses many different terms to refer to God's Word. Also, this psalm says a lot about being eager to know God's Word and being willing to respond to God's Word.

Read the psalm now. On a separate sheet of paper, record the different things the psalmist said that indicate his willingness to learn and to respond to God's Word. Also, see whether you can identify and list all of the different terms the psalmist used to refer to God's message. (Find ten in the King James Version.)

TERMS IN PSALM 119 THAT REFER TO GOD'S WORD

1. _____ 6. _____
2. _____ 7. _____
3. _____ 8. _____
4. _____ 9. _____
5. _____ 10. _____

We don't have enough space in this session to list all that the psalmist said to indicate his willingness to learn and to respond to God's Word. That's why I asked you to use a separate piece of paper. In Psalm 119:24 he shows his delight in the Word of God. It performs an important role of leadership in his life. The psalmist knows that he needs to understand what God has said. Psalm 119:34 is a prayer for this understanding. The words of Psalm 119:105 express again the role of God's Word in giving leadership. Psalm 119:108 expresses an openness, obedience, and willingness to learn. The last verse of the psalm expresses human weakness. The psalmist still recognizes that the commandments of the Lord are a solution to his problems. These are just a few of the references you may have found. There are many others in the psalm.

How many of the ten different terms did you find? Here is my list: words, precepts, judgments, commandments, statutes, law, ways, testimonies, ordinances, and path.

Throughout this psalm the writer shows a willingness to learn. He is teachable. God shows His truths and commandments to people who are teachable. God does not give spiritual understanding to a rebel. He gives spiritual understanding to His friends.

In John 15:14-15 Jesus describes His friends as those who do whatever He commands them. Jesus promises that He will teach His friends everything which He has learned from His Father. God's friends are those who are teachable and obedient. They alone will learn God's message in all of its richness.

Some factors can negatively affect a person's teachable attitude. Mark 4 records a parable Jesus used to identify three different factors that destroy our teachable attitude and keep us from being good Bible students. In the parable Jesus called these factors hard ground (the road), rocky ground, and thorny ground.

Study the parable and Jesus' interpretation in Mark 4:1-20. According to Jesus' interpretation, what are the three factors that destroy your teachable attitude?

The road = _____

The rocky ground = _____

The thorns = _____

Jesus said that some people are like hard soil because their receptivity to God's Word has been destroyed. He said other people are like a thin layer of soil over a shelf of rock because different factors have kept them from developing any spiritual depth in which the Word of God can take root and grow. He said the third group are like thorny soil because different factors choke out God's truth in our lives or distract us from it.

When I was growing up, my father tried to teach me how to do home repairs. I wasn't interested in learning to change faucet washers and electrical wall sockets. I preferred to play basketball with my friends. I wasn't teachable, and I didn't learn.

When I purchased my home, I began to ask how to do some of these home repairs. I was interested, open, and teachable. I began to learn what I had not learned. I had become teachable.

The fact that you are engaged in this study indicates that you want your life to be like the fourth group, whose lives are like deep, rich soil that received the seed of God's Word and produced an abundance of fruits. I want to encourage you to identify the roads and the rocky areas and the thorny areas in your life and begin right now at this session to make them a matter of prayer. Doing this may be frightening or frustrating to you because you do not even know how to begin. Perhaps you have identified these areas in your life and have been struggling with them for a long time—but without much success.

Encouragement and a promise are found in Hebrews 4:15-16. What does this passage promise you about your struggle to deal with the factors that try to destroy your teachable attitude?

_____

_____

Yes, God knows your struggles because in the person of Jesus He experienced those same struggles Himself, and He promises to help you. Imagine that! God is saying to you: "Yes, I know. I have been there Myself. I will help you."

What does the passage say you need to do to get the help you need?

_____

That's right. You need to go to God without fear or hesitation and claim His promise of help.

By the way, you have just read your second Scripture memory assignment—Hebrews 4:16. By this time you should have 1 Corinthians 2:14 almost memorized. Get your next Scripture memory card and begin memorizing your new assignment.

17

WEEK 1, DAY 4

THIS UNIT: One Prerequisite for Bible Study
TODAY: Dependence on the Holy Spirit

Read John 16:13-15; 1 John 2:27.

The Bible is hard for some people to understand. They come to the Bible with a faulty attitude. They are defeated even before they study the Bible. This is what they think: *The Bible contains such hard words and difficult ideas. It won't make sense to me.*

Other people come to the study of the Bible with a vibrant attitude. They know that God wants them to understand the Bible's message. They are excited and think: *God can speak clearly to me as I study the Bible. The Holy Spirit can give me insight into the message.*

A Christian can be excited as he comes to study the Bible because he does have the Holy Spirit. The Holy Spirit comes into the Christian when he becomes a child of God. The Holy Spirit is a God-given teacher for making the Bible real and applicable. You read in John 16:13-15 that one specific task the Holy Spirit has in the world is to teach you all the things that God wants you to know. Imagine that! God Himself in the person of the Holy Spirit is beside you each time you open your Bible to study, and He will personally show you all the things He wants you to know about Himself. That is something you can really get excited about when you sit down to study God's Word.

By this time you should have committed 1 Corinthians 2:14 to memory. Write the verse here.

The verse you have written is part of a passage that says some important things about the Holy Spirit's role as a teacher. Read 1 Corinthians 2:10-14 and check the phrase that you think best completes each of the following statements.
1. God uses the Holy Spirit to be our teacher because
   ☐ the Holy Spirit can be every place at the same time.
   ☐ the Holy Spirit knows the deep truths of God.
   ☐ the Holy Spirit has a college education.
2. The only way a person can learn the things of God is to
   ☐ meditate constantly on God.
   ☐ learn them from the Spirit of God.
   ☐ believe every word in the Bible.
3. We are able to receive the truth of God because
   ☐ God loves us more than any other persons in the world.
   ☐ we have received the Spirit of God.
   ☐ our Bible is the King James Version.
4. The truth of God is foolish to a person who is not a Christian because
   ☐ that person does not have the advantage of regular Bible study and worship.
   ☐ that person has not received the Holy Spirit.
   ☐ people who are not Christians have a strange sense of humor.

Well, I hope you checked the second choice in each case. Some of the options were meant to make you think, and others were meant to make you smile. However, in each case, I think the second choice is the correct one. Can you write in one sentence what you think is the main teaching of 1 Corinthians 2:10-14?

Now, read again 1 John 2:27. The anointing John spoke of in this verse is the anointing of the Holy Spirit. But is John actually saying that we do not need any resource other than the Holy Spirit to know the truth of God? Surely not. This verse must be considered with other verses such as Proverbs 1:2-5. Read that verse. Think carefully and decide what John was saying. (A commentary will help you at this point.)

What sort of information does the Holy Spirit teach? He won't provide biblical facts which you can learn in a Bible dictionary. He won't, for example, teach the difference between the Amorites and the Amalekites. He won't provide a solution to some disputed biblical facts. For example, you won't learn the identity of the author of Hebrews by depending on the Holy Spirit.

The Holy Spirit will shape your attitudes and spiritual perception. He will develop within you a spiritually receptive outlook. He will heighten your intellect so that you can understand some of the doctrines of the Bible.

The role of the Holy Spirit is to illuminate the Bible. He makes you wise about the contents of the Bible. He doesn't take you beyond it. He is not in the business of giving revelation in addition to or contrary to the Bible. He builds on what is there and makes its meaning and application clear. I think it is fair to say that the Holy Spirit is our ultimate and final teacher. No person can truthfully teach us anything that is contrary to the Holy Spirit or that the Holy Spirit is not willing to verify as true. In a very real sense all other persons, objects, printed materials, opinions, and so on are merely resources, and the Holy Spirit is the one who uses those resources to teach us about God.

As you study the Bible, you should not claim to be error free in your opinions because of the leadership of the Holy Spirit. A Christian should avoid saying, "The Holy Spirit has shown me this solution, and that's the way it is!" Humility and meekness must replace pride and arrogance in attitude.

How can you find the strength of the Holy Spirit in Bible study? You must begin the study with a prayer for guidance. Those Bible students who have been able to understand the Bible and teach others have always mixed prayers generously with their studies. Have you seen any sample in the Bible of prayers for understanding the Bible? If you remember Psalm 119, you can recall that it contains many such prayers. Read again some of these prayers and make them a sample of the kind of request which you will make as you begin your study of the Bible.

As you begin the study of the Bible, recognize that you have no reason to feel defeated. God has given you the best possible teacher in the Holy Spirit. God desires that you be positive and excited about the study of the Bible. Your dependence on the Holy Spirit can bring this attitude into your own Bible study.

WEEK 1, DAY 5

THIS UNIT: One Prerequisite for Bible Study
TODAY: Discipline

Read 2 Timothy 2:15.

Today you complete your first week of *How to Study Your Bible*. Do you remember the subject or theme that you have been studying this week? Write it on the thumb of the hand diagram in the next column.

All this week you have been learning that **ONE PREREQUISITE** for being a serious student of the Bible is having a spiritual hunger for the Word of God. And you have been learning what is necessary to create and to maintain that spiritual hunger. Today you will see how discipline in your study habits is necessary if you are to maintain a spiritual hunger for God's Word.

Professional athletes train and practice for years to perform their sport in peak condition. Professional musicians practice for hours each day to develop their ability to its highest level. The study of the Bible also demands discipline and hard work. A Christian cannot learn God's truths, commands, and promises by sitting back and expecting the Holy Spirit to program him with truth.

What do you suppose Paul was urging Timothy to do in 2 Timothy 2:15? Read this verse in at least one contemporary translation or paraphrase. If you have added a commentary to your personal library of study resources, do a study of this verse. Then write on a separate sheet of paper what you think Paul was saying and how that applies to you. Do this before you read the next paragraph.

The words Paul used describe hard work and mighty effort. Your written statement should convey the idea that Christians are expected to work hard at developing their ability to interpret God's

Word correctly and to apply it correctly.

A Christian needs a disciplined attitude in order to learn the Bible. There are new words to learn. There are new thoughts about God to understand and apply. The Bible has customs which we don't practice in our culture. Understanding them is vital to understanding the Bible. The Bible speaks about events which we haven't heard of before. Understanding them is important in interpreting the Bible. You must be disciplined to be a good Bible student.

A Christian must have discipline in order to continue to study the Bible. High-school and college students must find time to study the Bible just as they have to find time to master history or calculus. Homemakers must find time to study the Bible in addition to cleaning the house and caring for a child. Persons who work in business or industry must find time to study the Bible as they face the daily pressures of commuting and carrying a heavy work load. Parents must find time for Bible study in addition to finding time for each other and their children. You must have discipline to continue to study the Bible.

All parts of the Bible are important. All parts of the Bible aren't equally interesting. All parts of the Bible are not equally clear. Many people have pledged to study and learn the Bible, but they quit as they study some of the books. Some have stopped when they reach Leviticus, and others stumble over Revelation. These books are difficult. They are, however, relevant. You must have the discipline to persevere in order to understand the difficult sections of the Bible.

Interpreting the Bible demands skills. It is not just learning a set of inflexible rules. Understanding the Bible requires common sense and judgment. These qualities come only from experience. A professional pianist understands just which mood to show in performing the music of a noted composer. A professional football player can use his experience to perceive the other team's plans for the next play. Understanding the Bible demands making choices among different interpretations. This is a skill which demands much experience. To interpret the Bible, you must study diligently.

The next ten weeks of this study will focus on helping you develop and practice necessary skills for correctly interpreting and applying God's Word. Let's look back on this week of study before we bring it to an end. Review with our friend in the illustration the necessary elements in creating and maintaining a spiritual hunger for God's Word. Make an honest estimate of the areas in which you need improvement. Engage in a time of prayer in which you commit yourself to hard work and disciplined study during the next ten weeks.

WEEK 2, DAY 1

***THIS UNIT:** Two Rules to Guide Bible Study*
***THIS TOPIC:** Rule 1—Use the Right Guidelines for Interpreting the Bible*
***TODAY:** Understand the Writer's Meaning*

Read Psalm 119:105; Matthew 7:3-4; Mark 9:33-37.

Today you begin the second major area in your study. Look at the hand diagram in the next column to see what that area is.

In this unit you will learn how to apply these two rules to guide Bible study.
1. Use the right guidelines for interpreting the Bible.
2. Use correct principles for applying the Bible.

Interpreting the Bible is an art and a science. A science has rules and guidelines which describe its content. The interpretation of the Bible requires some guidelines to understand its content. To apply these guidelines demands wisdom and experience, and this is an art. A Bible student practices the art of interpretation when he uses the right guideline in the right way.

We will learn five guidelines which will help us in our interpretation of the Bible. These guidelines will help us to grasp the meaning of the Bible. When we have understood what the Bible means, we will need help to apply the Bible to daily life. We will learn some principles to help us to apply the Bible in our experiences.

Today you will study the first of five guidelines for interpreting the

Bible: **UNDERSTAND THE WRITER'S MEANING.** I want to share with you two keys to understanding what the writer meant to say. The first key is **DISCOVER THE WRITER'S LITERAL MEANING.** Across the centuries, some Bible students have chosen to ignore the literal meaning of a Scripture and have looked for an allegorical meaning. These students have tried to move from the literal meaning to a deeper, spiritual meaning. By taking this approach, these students often read meanings into the Scriptures that were never intended by the writer.

The Bible does have deep, spiritual meanings; but the goal of the serious Bible student is to begin by discovering what the writer was trying to say.

The other key I want to share with you is **UNDERSTAND FIGURES OF SPEECH.** A passage of Scripture might have some elements which we cannot interpret literally. Psalm 91:4 describes God in these words: "He shall cover thee with his feathers, and under his wings shalt thou trust" (KJV). If we take the literal meaning, should we say that God has feathers and wings? No, because the psalmist is using a figure of speech called a metaphor.

To understand the metaphor, we will observe that the psalmist is using a figure of speech. We then seek the meaning of the figure of speech. The language used describes how a hen covers her chicks with feathers and wings. God doesn't have feathers and wings, but He does have love and is strong. The psalmist was describing the love and protection of the Father. Since poetic writings like Psalms often have figures of speech, we should be alert for these expressions as we read poetic books.

Now I want you to work with some figures of speech. A commentary will be helpful. You may want to talk with your pastor or some other experienced Bible student. Study each passage listed on the chart. Then write in the left column what you think the writer meant by what he said. (For the time being, leave the right column blank.)

What the writer said	Applications
Psalm 119:105	
Mark 9:33-37	
Matthew 7:3-4	

When we interpret the Bible, we must look for the normal, obvious meaning. This is the literal meaning. A passage of Scripture will have only one literal meaning. We may disagree over what the literal meaning actually is, but only one of the possible meanings can be correct.

Even though there is only one literal meaning, there are many possible applications of a passage. The application is the use of the passage made in daily life. There can be many of these applications. They all must be based on the single meaning, but there can be many of them. Now go back to the chart. Based on your understanding of the writer's meaning in each passage, write at least two ways to apply each passage to your life.

Read Ephesians 4:32. Notice what it teaches about the motivation behind forgiveness. Can you think of different situations in which you might apply this passage? Memorize this passage as one of your verses for this week.

WEEK 2, DAY 2

THIS UNIT: *Two Rules to Guide Bible Study*
THIS TOPIC: *Rule 1—Use the Right Guidelines for Interpreting the Bible*
TODAY: *Observe the Context*

Read Luke 10:25-37; John 9:3; Philippians 4:4.

Yesterday we learned that the Bible should be interpreted literally. We learned that interpreting some passages might require that we take the symbolic meaning of a figure of speech. We know also that a given passage of Scripture has one meaning but many possible applications.

Another important guideline in Bible interpretation is to **OBSERVE THE CONTEXT.** The context will refer to at least two separate things. One part of the context is the section in the Bible where a given verse or passage appears. Another part of the context is to observe the culture or circumstances in which the event or statement occurred.

The biblical context of a statement or verse will refer to the verses surrounding the statement. It also may refer to the context of an entire book. This wider context is sometimes crucial in understanding the Bible's meaning.

To understand the importance of the biblical context, read John 9:3. Notice the startling statement by Jesus "neither that this man sinned, nor his parents." Could this "sinless" man be descended from a "sinless" family?

To understand verse 3, you must read it in context with verses 1 and 2. Consider the verse in context and write in the box what you think Jesus was saying when He made this statement.

[ ]

Jesus was not discussing the subject of sinlessness either at birth or in life. He was discussing whether or not the blindness of the man was due to sin by somebody. Jesus said that the blindness of the man was not due to his own sin nor to that of his parents. A closer reading of surrounding verses can prevent a serious misunderstanding of Scripture.

Let's look at another passage. Luke 14:26 records that Jesus said you cannot be His disciple unless you hate your parents and your children and all the other persons who are dear to you. Could that possibly be true? Read Luke 14:15-35 to see the verse in context. Then write in the box what you think Jesus was saying.

[ ]

When Jesus spoke these words, He was on the way to the cross. Once again, He was trying to stress to His followers in the most vivid terms possible the degree of devotion that discipleship demands and the importance of counting the cost of discipleship. There must be no other love in life that compares to our love for Him.

The context of the Bible will refer also to the culture or circumstances in which a given event or statement appears. A knowledge of biblical social customs, history, or geography can help greatly in the interpretation of the Bible. A knowledge of the circumstances under which a writer spoke will illuminate his statements. You will need help discovering the social and cultural context of a passage. A commentary, a New Testament survey or introduction, and a Bible dictionary are helpful tools in understanding the context of a verse.

Read Paul's joy-filled words in Philippians 4:4. His statement is: "Rejoice in the Lord always; again I will say, rejoice!" What makes this exhortation from Paul special? Discover where Paul was and the conditions under which he was living. Write your explanation in the box.

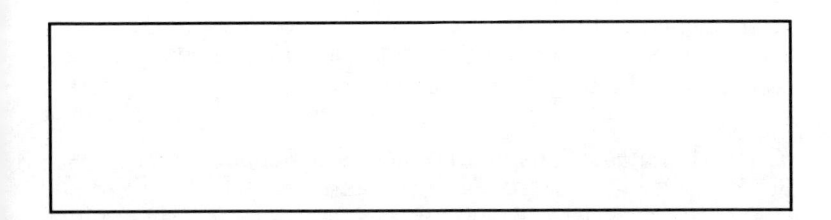

Paul was not living under the best conditions when he wrote this, was he? Paul's reference to the "guard" and his "imprisonment" in Philippians 1:13 suggests that he was under arrest. Perhaps it was not a situation like solitary confinement. But it was certainly not a peaceful, comfortable life. He was likely chained to a guard and was confined to the cramped location of his own house (Acts 28:30).

When Paul urged his readers to express their joy, his circumstances were not easy. He was under arrest and confined. If Paul could be joyful in this situation, the strength of God must be unbelievable! A knowledge of Paul's situation throws light on this passage.

Read the parable of the Good Samaritan in Luke 10:30-37. Jesus spoke these words to a prominent Jew who felt that he was one of God's favored people. In the parable a priest and a Levite refuse to help the wounded man. Their stopping would inconvenience them. Only the Samaritan sacrificed himself for the wounded man. What was special about this act of mercy? Discover the context and write an explanation in the box.

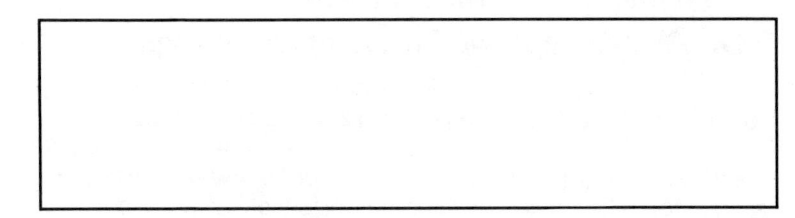

To understand fully the impact of this story on the Jews of Jesus' time, we must know how they viewed the Samaritans. The Samaritans were a mixed-race people who practiced a religion with a combination of Judaism and paganism. They were hated and despised by the Jews. It was unthinkable to a Jew that a Samaritan would show such mercy. The average Jew would not want this mercy from a Samaritan.

A knowledge of the context of this verse in the life of the Jewish people makes it clear and understandable in our own time.

As you read your Bible this week, be especially sensitive to the way the context of the verses should influence your understanding.

WEEK 2, DAY 3

THIS UNIT: *Two Rules to Guide Bible Study*
THIS TOPIC: *Rule 1—Use the Right Guidelines for Interpreting the Bible*
TODAY: *Accept the Limits of Revelation*

Read Mark 13:32; 2 Corinthians 12:9-10; 1 Peter 3:1.

Today you reach the midpoint of your second week of study. You should now have three Scriptures committed to memory. From memory, write the three references here.

_____ _____

_____

Now, quickly recite those Scriptures aloud. If another person is available, ask that person to use your Scripture memory cards to check you. Begin today to memorize Matthew 21:22.

Recall that in this unit we are studying two rules to guide Bible study. This week we are studying rule 1, which is **USE THE RIGHT GUIDELINES FOR INTERPRETING THE BIBLE.** You have already studied and practiced using two of those guidelines: (1) understand the writer's meaning and (2) observe the context. Today you will study the third guideline: **ACCEPT THE LIMITS OF REVELATION.**

Where God has spoken in the Bible, He has spoken accurately and truthfully. However, the Bible has not spoken on all subjects of interest to us. Sometimes a Bible student attempts to strain from the Bible more information than God has put there.

The primary purpose of the Bible is to outline God's plan for man's redemption through Christ. The Bible is not a textbook of medicine or science. The Bible is not concerned with predicting the arrival of spaceships or completely outlining the way in which the world is to end. We must remember the primary purpose of the Bible as we seek to understand its meaning.

Even when the Bible speaks concerning our redemption and other topics of spiritual interest, God has not told us all we may want to know. He has shared in the Bible all that is necessary for our spiritual needs. We must be content with this information and not try to push beyond it.

If you are like me, you still have quite a few questions for which you would like to be able to find biblical answers. And if you are like me, you have not yet found answers that are completely satisfactory. What are some of your questions? Write them in or around the question mark in the diagram on the next page.

One of the most widespread promises of Scripture is that Jesus Christ will return again bodily. Such passages as Titus 2:12-13 and 1 Thessalonians 4:13-18 gloriously describe this event. However, the Bible has not provided a clear outline of the chronology of Jesus' return. A reading of Mark 13:32 shows that even Jesus Himself did not know the exact hour of His return at the time that He spoke these words. A verse such as this should warn us against predicting that Jesus is going to come in our lifetime. It should warn us against rigidly arranging the events which will occur when Jesus returns. We must not view our opinion as God's final word on the subject.

The Bible does not describe fully the factors which cause tragedy and suffering. It is spiritually unwise to use Scripture to prove God's purposes in allowing a given event. Paul learned that God had permitted his "thorn in the flesh" in order to teach him more complete dependence on the Lord (2 Cor. 12:9-10). However, this was a personal assurance given to Paul. The cause of much suffering is a mystery. We can be certain that the strength of God can enable us to endure suffering (Jas. 1:2-4). We must be careful in using the Bible to show to a suffering Christian what God is trying to do in his life.

Sometimes the teaching about the relationship of Christian wives to their husbands is distorted by the misuse of the Bible. Some have used the Bible to suggest that the Christian wife always must follow her husband even if it leads into sin, into disobedience, or away from the church. Observe how Peter deals with this subject in 1 Peter 3:1. Peter is urging that wives place themselves under their husbands specifically for the purpose of winning them to Christ. Peter is not talking about absolute obedience to an overbearing husband. He is describing how a Christian wife may influence her non-Christian husband to Christ. It is going beyond the Bible to suggest that the Bible teaches that the wife must obey the husband even if it leads her to disobey God. Peter has an entirely different purpose in mind. He is outlining how to win a stubborn non-Christian husband to Christ. We must not press the Bible to say more than God has spoken.

You should cultivate the ability to be content to know only what God wants you to know. The serious Bible student does not find it necessary to demand from the Bible answers that are not there.

WEEK 2, DAY 4

THIS UNIT: *Two Rules to Guide Bible Study*
THIS TOPIC: *Rule 1—Use the Right*
  Guidelines for Interpreting the Bible
TODAY: *Identify the Type of Writing*

Read Isaiah 1:16; Acts 3:7; Colossians 4:3; Revelation 13:1.

The Bible contains many different types of writing. Some of the literature is Hebrew poetry. The Books of Psalms, Proverbs, and many of the Old Testament Prophets contain poetry. Writings of prophecy give a glimpse of what God will do in the future. The Old Testament Book of Daniel and the New Testament Book of Revelation are examples of prophetic writings. Narrative writings tell a story of what God has done in history. Genesis and Exodus in the Old Testament and the Gospels (Matthew, Mark, Luke, and John) and Acts in the New Testament are narratives. The New Testament also has letters from Paul, Peter, and John. These letters teach God's message to young Christians. They are called epistles.

Some books of the Bible have several kinds of writing in the same book. Isaiah, for example, has poetry, prophecy, and narrative sections. However, any book will fit primarily into one category, although it may contain elements of other kinds of writings. The bookcase illustration will help you identify the primary classification of the writings in each book in the Bible.

To interpret the Bible properly, it is important to observe the kind of writing which you are reading. Poetry and prophecy have many figures of speech in their statements. You have already learned that you must be alert to figures of speech such as metaphors, and you must take care to understand what the writer is saying. If you have not added a commentary to your Bible study tools, I hope you are planning to do so soon. You really need a commentary to help you with the following exercises. Let's look now at some figures of speech in the Bible and practice discovering what the writer was actually saying.

Read Isaiah 1:16. This is Hebrew poetry, and most versions of the Bible will indicate this by setting the words in the form of poetry.

Notice the context of Isaiah's words. The prophet has described the rebellion of the children of Israel. Their prayers were empty. The people had turned against God. What does the writer say the solution is?

_____

Correct. The Scripture says that the people should wash themselves and make themselves clean. Are a bathtub and a bar of soap the solutions for the guilt of sin? Surely not! This must be a figure of speech. Use a commentary to discover what the writer is actually saying. Write your interpretation here.

_____

The figure of speech in Isaiah 1:16 calls for repentance, spiritual cleansing, and fresh commitment to God. This cleansing does not require soap and water. It demands confession and forsaking sin.

Read Revelation 13:1. John pictures a wild beast who leads human beings into evil. Who is this beast? Is it a creature such as you might see in a zoo? Is it a symbol for the evil power of the Roman Empire? Is it a picture of an evil human being in the last times? We are safe to say that this is not a zoo animal. It is harder to choose between the other two options. Here it would be helpful to read a commentary on Revelation 13:1 to gain understanding. This is a prophetic passage, and the beast is a symbol. You probably need help to understand what the symbol means. Study the commentary again and write your interpretation here.

_____

Read Acts 3:7. This appears in a narrative passage. Luke, the writer of Acts, describes Peter's healing of a lame man. The man had been born with this problem. Peter healed him in the presence of a crowd of people. Did it happen as Luke says? Yes, Luke intends that we understand this as a miracle. It isn't that Peter touched the man and so inspired him with positive thinking that he could get up and walk on his own. By the power of Jesus Christ, Peter performed a miracle upon a man who was genuinely lame. This is narrative writing. We will make a simple, literal interpretation of this type of writing. Although the narrative books and the epistles are to be taken more literally than prophecy and poetry, these books too contain occasional figures of speech that must be interpreted. Read Colossians 4:3. This book is a letter from Paul to the church at Colossae asking for prayer for his work. Do you see a figure of speech in verse 3? Identify the figure of speech, decide how it should be interpreted, and write your answer here.

_____

The figure of speech is the word *door*, and it represents an opportunity to preach Christ. Paul asks his readers to pray that God would provide him an opportunity to preach Christ.

When you read the Bible, observe the kind of writing which you read. If the writing is poetry or prophecy, be alert to interpret properly the many figures of speech. If the writing is narrative or a letter, interpret the writing more literally.

Begin the second Scripture memory assignment for this week—Matthew 21:22.

29

WEEK 2, DAY 5

THIS UNIT: Two Rules to Guide Bible Study
THIS TOPIC: Rule 1—Use the Right Guidelines for Interpreting the Bible
TODAY: Use the Bible to Interpret Itself

Read Matthew 21:22; John 14:13; James 4:3; 1 John 5:14-15.

Today you complete the second week in your study, and this is a good time to review. Write on the first finger of the hand diagram in the next column the unit that you are studying.

The unit you are studying is **TWO RULES TO GUIDE BIBLE STUDY.** The first rule is:

USE THE RIGHT G_____ FOR
I_____ THE BIBLE.

Today you will study the fifth guideline: **USE THE BIBLE TO INTERPRET ITSELF.** Many passages of the Bible will not be easy to understand. Often these hard passages become clearer when another passage of the Bible can help to explain them. We can use the Bible to explain itself. A clearer passage in the Bible can help to clarify a difficult passage. A simple statement can make more sense than a complex statement. The Bible is its own best interpreter.

Many subjects in the Bible are discussed in more than one passage of the Bible. Sometimes the Bible discusses a subject briefly in one section and more fully in another section. We always should use the more detailed discussion as we seek to understand the Bible.

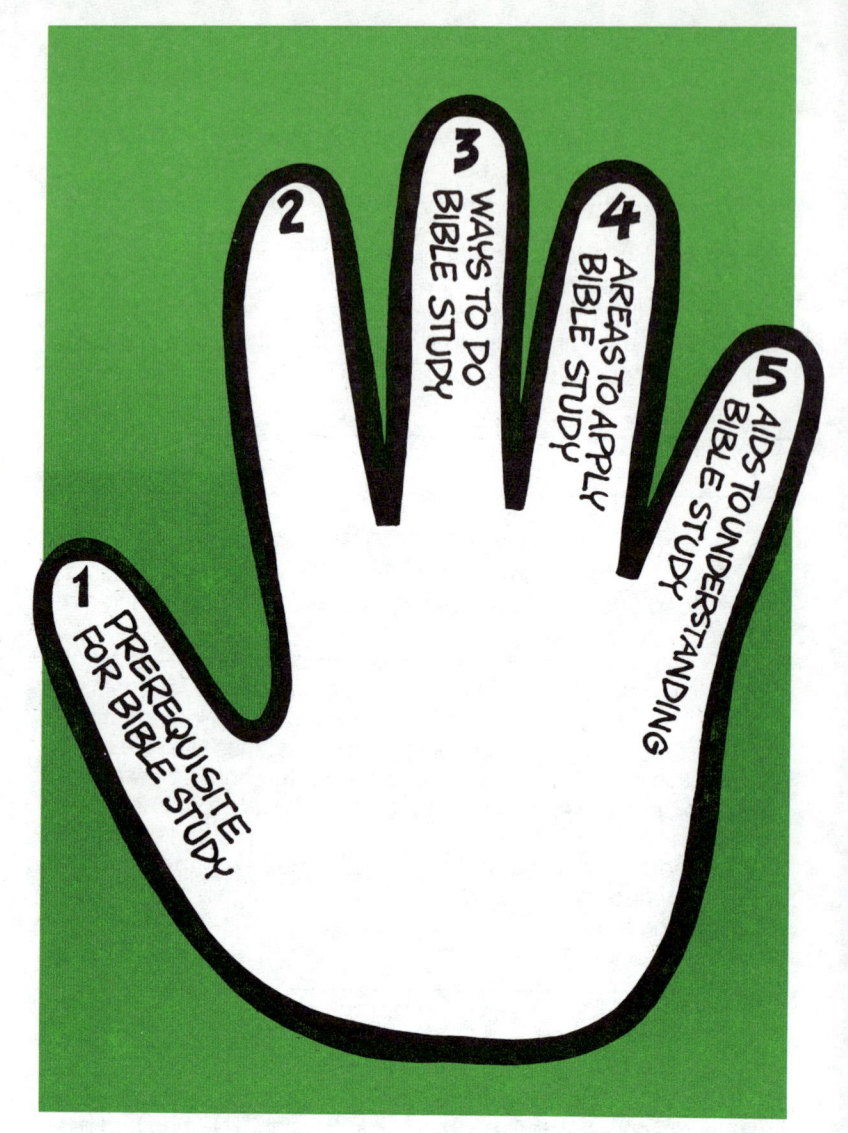

It is true that one mention of a truth or a commandment in the Bible is enough to make it important. However, that one mention of the truth may not be clear. In this case we shouldn't use the unclear passage to teach firm doctrine. Paul makes a reference in 1 Corinthians 15:29 to those who "are baptized for the dead." This seems to suggest that one person can be baptized for another person. Such an idea would contradict the rest of the Bible. Baptism is always an experience which a Christian undergoes to express *his own* faith in Christ. The exact meaning of this passage is not clear. It is clear, however, that it does not suggest proxy baptism. Such a meaning would be contrary to other passages of the Bible (Acts 8:36; 1 Pet. 3:21).

To develop important doctrine and teachings, it is best to use those passages of the Bible which fully discuss the doctrine. For example, the resurrection of Christ is discussed fully in 1 Corinthians 15. The nature of faith is discussed in Hebrews 11. It would be important to use these passages in a study of these subjects.

Now practice using the Bible to interpret the Bible. Read Matthew 21:22. A careless reading of this passage may lead a person to believe that he can get anything he wants from God if he has enough faith. But hold on a minute. In addition to the passage in Matthew, you were assigned to read three other passages at the beginning of this session. Review those passages and write a brief summary of what the Bible says to interpret Matthew 21:22.

_____

_____

_____

James 4:3 shows you that God will not answer prayer if your motive is selfish. God says in 1 John 5:14-15 that His own will is the important factor in receiving an answer in prayer. Faith alone will not guarantee that God will grant a request. Some of these requests might not be in God's will. John 14:13 states the same truth. When we pray, we must seek the will of God and not our own wishes.

When we want to understand what the Bible teaches on a subject such as prayer, we must consider the entire Bible. If we consider only one single passage, we might reach a wrong conclusion. We must use the Bible to interpret itself. It is its own best interpreter.

Matthew 21:22 shows the importance of faith in God in receiving an answer to prayer. It does not teach that you can get anything from God if you will only believe. Obedience to God, a desire for God's will, and good motives must be your concern if you want God to answer your prayers.

Now you should know five guidelines for interpreting Scripture. Can you list them?

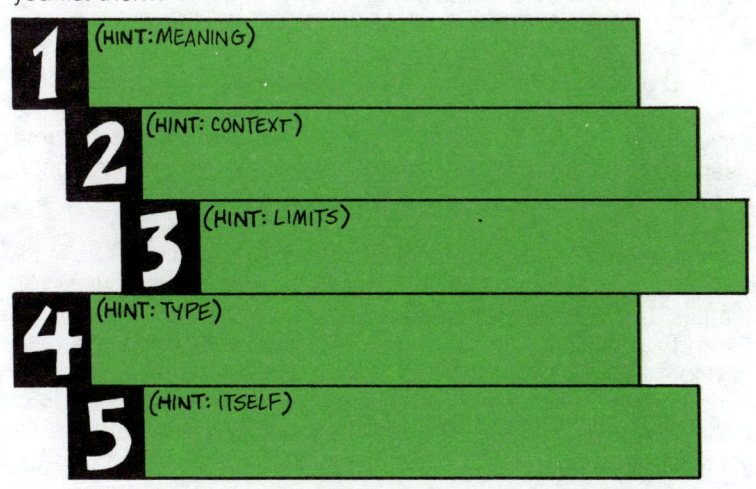

1 (HINT: MEANING)

2 (HINT: CONTEXT)

3 (HINT: LIMITS)

4 (HINT: TYPE)

5 (HINT: ITSELF)

If you had difficulty listing the guidelines, review the headings at the beginning of the sessions for this week. Your assignment for tomorrow is to make thorough preparation for your weekend at church.

WEEK 3, DAY 1

THIS UNIT: *Two Rules to Guide Bible Study*
THIS TOPIC: *Rule 2—Use Correct Principles for Applying the Bible*
TODAY: *Apply the Bible According to Its Real Meaning*

Read Ephesians 4:26; 1 Thessalonians 5:17; 1 Timothy 5:23; 1 Peter 3:6.

This week you will continue studying two rules to guide Bible study. Last week you studied rule 1: **USE THE RIGHT GUIDELINES FOR INTERPRETING THE BIBLE.** This week you will study rule 2: **USE CORRECT PRINCIPLES FOR APPLYING THE BIBLE.**

A group of young Christians from an Ethiopian tribe were visiting in a missionary home. One of the missionary's children bounded into the living room. The family dog was right behind. The small dog came near the visitors in a friendly fashion. The guests retreated in apparent fear.

The missionary felt they were fearful. "He won't harm you," he reassured them about the dog. The guests replied that they were not fearful. They had felt that Christians were not to have dogs around them. Their biblical support for this belief was Paul's word to "beware of dogs" (Phil. 3:2, KJV). The missionary explained that Paul had in mind human beings who acted like dirty, vicious street dogs.[1] Paul had nothing against dogs. The zealous young Christians had used a verse but had given it the wrong meaning.

Whenever we apply a verse in our life, we must use it in accordance with its meaning. The first goal of a Bible student is to learn what the verse means. Then the student must apply it in life based on what that verse really means. Each of the four verses you read at the beginning of this session could be misapplied by a person who did not understand the real meaning of the verse. Your assignment for this session is to discover the real meaning of each verse and write a brief statement of how you can apply that verse in your life based on its real meaning. Modern English translations, a commentary, and other Bible study tools will be helpful to you.

Is Paul saying in Ephesians 4:26 that Christians should develop their ability to be angry? Discover the real meaning of this verse.

```
How I can apply Ephesians 4:26 in my life.



```

Paul recognized there is such a thing as righteous anger. People will become indignant over their own treatment or the treatment of others. It might be wrong not to be indignant. It also would be wrong to allow the indignation to rise out of control. Indignation over wrong might lead to action based on wounded pride or personal resentment. This would be sinful. Paul is saying to you: "If you get angry, don't let this lead you into sinful acts. Keep your anger under control." Knowing the meaning of the verse helps you to apply it.

In 1 Thessalonians 5:17 did Paul instruct Christians to pray without a break? Are we never to take time to eat, sleep, or read the Bible? Discover the real meaning of the verse.

---

[1]. Raymond Davis, *Fire on the Mountains* (SIM International, Toronto, 1980), 112. Used by permission.

> How I can apply 1 Thessalonians 5:17 in my life.

In your study you should have discovered that to pray without ceasing means that you should be continually in an attitude of prayer. Paul does not mean that you should pray so that you never eat, sleep, or read the Bible. He wants the attitude of prayer to be constantly within you. He doesn't want you to feel guilty if you are not praying. There are other important actions in the Christian life besides prayer.

Should you use 1 Timothy 5:23 as a basis for drinking alcoholic beverages? Discover the real meaning of the verse.

> How I can apply 1 Timothy 5:23 in my life.

To understand what Paul means, we must notice the situation concerning water, and we must observe the purpose for drinking the wine. Water in Paul's day was often impure. Drinking that water could make Timothy sick. Wine in Paul's day could be used as a medicine. That is the purpose which Paul had in mind. He was not telling Timothy to use wine as a beverage. He is telling him to use wine as a medicine to treat his stomach problems.

Was Peter suggesting in 1 Peter 3:6 that a Christian wife view her husband as an army private views his company commander? Discover the real meaning of the verse.

> How I can apply 1 Peter 3:6 in my life.

You probably discovered that Peter spoke of the respect that husbands and wives should have for each other. Such respect will lead the wife to hear and follow the suggestions of the husband rather than looking at him as a foolish bumbler. Notice that Peter urged the husband to give the same respect to the wife in 3:7. Peter's purpose was to commend Sarah's respect for Abraham. He didn't intend that Sarah or a modern wife treat her husband like a field marshall.

I hope you are working at your Scripture memorization each day. Periodically reviewing all the verses you have memorized is very important. Otherwise, you will begin to lose them from your mental memory bank. Today you should begin memorizing 1 Peter 5:7.

WEEK 3, DAY 2

THIS UNIT: *Two Rules to Guide Bible Study*
THIS TOPIC: *Rule 2—Use Correct Principles for Applying the Bible*
TODAY: *Use the Bible as a Book of Principles*

Read Acts 2:42-45; 1 Corinthians 8:13; James 2:1-7.

The Bible contains many principles which show us how to live and serve God. The Bible warns us against many acts and attitudes which hinder our life and service for God. The directions and guidelines which the Bible gives are not detailed and specific. They are general and broad.

If the Bible were too specific in its warnings, it would be limited to one time and culture. If the Bible were a group of specific rules for every occasion, we might obey the letter of the rules and miss the genuine spirit of godly living. God intends that we struggle to apply His principles in our lives.

Read Acts 2:42-45. Here Luke, the author of Acts, describes Christians who sold their private belongings and gave them to Christian friends. Should we do the same today? Is it wrong for a Christian to have private property?

First, notice that Luke did not command us to copy what these early Christians did. He presented their examples, but he didn't command us to imitate it. Also, do you remember the principle of using the Bible to interpret itself? No other passages in the Bible command the Christian to sell his own property and give it to the poor. Many passages call upon Christians to be unselfish and generous (Jas. 5:1-5; 1 John 3:17).

This spirit of generosity was due to the high sense of unity which the Holy Spirit had produced in the church. The rich members made a provision for the poorer members from their wealth. For a brief time no one could complain of hunger or general need. When the sense of unity died down, some Christians pretended to share their goods but actually did not (Acts 5:1-11). There is nothing wrong with owning property. However, we must be generous and avoid hypocrisy about our generosity.

Luke was showing the generosity and unselfishness of the early church. He was not commanding that we sell our own private property or feel guilty for having private goods. He was reminding us that we must be eager to share with the needy.

Read 1 Corinthians 8:13. Here Paul said that he would stop eating meat if that offended his fellow Christians. What has meat to do with the Christian life? Is it wrong for us to eat meat?

A commentary on 1 Corinthians will help to explain the issue which Paul faced. Early Christians could purchase meat to eat from an idol temple in their city. This meat had been part of a sacrifice to a pagan god. The unburned part of the sacrifice could be sold for eating. The meat was reasonable in price and tasty.

This practice offended some Christians. They felt that eating this meat was sinful. They didn't eat it, and they didn't want others to eat it. If they saw Paul eating such meat, his example would harm them.

Paul knew all of this and decided not to eat meat. The principle was that he would not do anything which harmed the spiritual life of another Christian. There is nothing wrong in itself with eating meat. However, if any action of yours proves harmful to another Christian, you should avoid it. That is Paul's principle and our use of it today.

Read James 2:1-7. What was James discussing? Again, a commentary on James would help us see the problem.

The Christians in James 2 were giving rich people the best seats in their meetings and telling the poor to find their own seats on the floor. It was a clear sense of bias against the poor and toward the rich. James called this sin. He stated the principle that Christians must not be biased for the rich and against the poor.

The Bible is not a book of detailed rules. It provides principles and broad guidelines which Christians should follow. As we seek to apply the Bible's teaching, we must learn and apply the principle which the Bible is teaching.

Now you see what I mean about looking for the broad, general directions and guidelines in the Bible and deriving principles for Christian living from those directions and guidelines. Let's see how you can do.

Study James 5:14-15. Identify the broad general guidelines. Draw from those guidelines a principle for Christian living. Then use that principle to respond to each of the following statements. In the box beside each statement put an *A* if your principle agrees with the statement; put a *D* if your principle disagrees; put a question mark if you are not sure.
- ☐ Christians have a responsibility to pray for and to minister to the sick.
- ☐ Christians with a strong belief in the healing power of God do not need doctors.
- ☐ God is the person who causes healing to take place.
- ☐ Christians make better doctors than non-Christians.
- ☐ Physical healing cannot take place apart from spiritual healing.
- ☐ Prayers for healing are effective only if the person being prayed for is a Christian.
- ☐ God can cause healing to take place in response to prayers of faith, without the assistance of doctors.
- ☐ If enough Christians had enough faith, sickness could be eradicated from the world.

Now study Mark 9:33-37 and respond to the following statements.
- ☐ We should seek out not those who can do things for us, but those who need us.
- ☐ Ambition and the desire to achieve are inconsistent with commitment to Christ.
- ☐ True greatness is in how much we serve, not in how much we are served.
- ☐ Jesus loves children more than He loves adults.
- ☐ The more power and influence a person has, the more difficult it is to be a committed Christian.
- ☐ A concern for self and a concern for serving others are inconsistent and cannot coexist in the life of a committed Christian.

WEEK 3, DAY 3

THIS UNIT: *Two Rules to Guide Bible Study*
THIS TOPIC: *Rule 2—Use Correct Principles for Applying the Bible*
TODAY: *Use the Promises Properly*

Read Joshua 1:9; John 3:16; James 4:8; 1 Peter 5:7.

"Every promise of the Bible is mine." Have you heard this from someone? It is not true. There are at least four different kinds of promises in the Bible. When we are dealing with any promise in the Bible, we must be careful to understand what kind of promise it is, and we must exercise caution in the way we apply that promise to our lives or to the lives of others. Let's look at these four different kinds of promises.

Some promises are universal. Some promises in the Bible apply equally to all persons. For example, general appeals to trust Christ are intended for all people. John 3:16 is an illustration of such an appeal.

Some promises are limited to God's people. The promises may appear to offer comfort to those who are not Christians, but they apply in their fullest sense to Christians. Peter urged his readers to cast all their concern upon God (1 Pet. 5:7). God's care for them was the encouragement to do this. These words sound good to use with all people. However, they apply best to committed Christians. Those who are God's children can trust their worries to their Heavenly Father. Those who are not will lack the relationship to enjoy the command.

By this time you should have memorized 1 Peter 5:7, the first Scripture memory assignment for this week. This verse is a promise with a related exhortation. See whether you can write the verse from memory.

_____

_____

This promise is the key to overcoming worries that can defeat you.

Some promises are personal—intended for one specific person. Promises to any individual are not always for general use. God spoke the words of Joshua 1:9 to Joshua alone. This mighty general was about to lead the children of Israel into the Promised Land. A series of mighty battles lay ahead. Joshua and his people needed God's encouragement for the struggle. God promised to be with them. Soldiers entering battle today can hope for God's presence with their cause. They cannot command God to act as He did with Joshua.

Some promises are conditional. A conditional promise is good only if the person to whom the promise is made meets some condition specified with the promise. James 4:8 is such a promise. James is saying that God comes near to those who seek Him. In the same way 1 Peter 5:6 contains a condition. God will exalt or glorify us only if we humble ourselves under the circumstances which He sends into our lives. The experience of the promise depends on the fulfillment of God's condition.

Now I want to give you some promises from the Bible to file away for future use, but it is important that you file them properly so that you can use them properly in the future. Study each promise in the following list and then list that promise on one of the folders in the Promise File illustration. I have done one or two to get you started.

John 3:16	2 Chronicles 7:14	1 Corinthians 10:13
Joshua 1:9	John 15:26	Matthew 7:7
John 14:6	1 Peter 5:7	Luke 1:20
Hebrews 13:5	James 4:8	Luke 13:13

UNIVERSAL

CONTENTS
1. JOHN 3:16
2. _____
3. _____

LIMITED

CONTENTS
1. 1 PETER 5:7
2. _____
3. _____

PERSONAL

CONTENTS
1. JOSHUA 1:9
2. _____
3. _____

CONDITIONAL

CONTENTS
1. JAMES 4:8
2. _____
3. _____

Abusing the promises of the Bible is a problem for the sincere Christian. Sometimes he eagerly wants God's guidance in his life and seeks it by opening the Bible without regard to the book he finds. He may take the first verse which he discovers as God's specific message to him. He may run the risk of finding a verse such as Colossians 3:5, which says, "Consider the members of your earthly body as dead." He also may find a verse such as Deuteronomy 33:8: "Let thy Thummim and thy Urim be with thy holy one" (KJV). The first verse is misleading, and the second is confusing.

Sometimes a sincere Christian becomes concerned about the physical condition of a friend or loved one. In asking God to heal a sick friend, he may take a verse such as James 5:15, which promises health for a prayer offered in faith. Here we should use other passages of Scripture to understand James 5:15. Remember that 1 John 5:14-15 shows that the will of God is the most important factor in prayer. Although God's will is generally for health, it is not true that God always plans for all sick people to get well.

A sincere Christian must use the promises of the Bible wisely lest he abuse them. He must consider whether the promise is universal, personal, or conditional. Before you end this study session, you should begin memorizing your next memory assignment—Matthew 18:21-22.

WEEK 3, DAY 4

***THIS UNIT:** Two Rules to Guide Bible Study*
***THIS TOPIC:** Rule 2—Use Correct Principles for Applying the Bible*
***TODAY:** Use a Cross-Cultural Understanding*

Read Leviticus 18:1-30; John 13:1-17; 2 Corinthians 13:12; 1 Peter 2:18.

Some of the commands and directions of the Bible seem confusing today because they are based on the culture of the Bible. Often the biblical command shows an important principle or truth. It may be possible to practice the principle today but to modify the form in which we practice it. This technique shows again that the Bible is a book of principles rather than a catalog of specific rules and laws.

In 2 Corinthians 13:12 Paul urges his readers to "greet one another with a holy kiss." If Christian men and women greeted one another today in churches with holy kisses, we might misunderstand their actions. To say the least, their actions would make us uncomfortable.

However, there is a principle or truth here that you and I can apply in our own lives. What is the principle, and how can you apply it?

_____
_____
_____
_____

Paul is really urging his readers to show deep brotherly love for one another. We can show brotherly love with a warm, firm handshake. By replacing the kiss with a handshake or even a warm embrace, we have demonstrated the principle of brotherly love.

In 1 Peter 2:18 Peter directed slaves to submit themselves to their masters with all respect. Can we infer from this that we have permission from Peter to own slaves? Of course not! But there is a principle or truth. What is that principle, and how can you apply it in your life?

Peter is not approving slavery in this passage. However, he accepted the fact that slavery was a part of his culture and that some very fine Christians were slaves. The principle here is that an employee should respect and work hard for his employer. When an employee today practices honesty and appreciation for his employer, he is following Peter's commands.

John 13:1-17 records that Jesus washed the feet of His disciples and urged them to wash one another's feet. Should Christians accept this incident as a biblical example that should be followed today? Not necessarily. But there is a principle we can apply to our lives. What is the principle, and how can you apply it to your life?

Foot washing in Jesus' day was usually done by a servant. Jesus and His disciples were meeting in the upper room for the Last Supper. When they came in from the street, they needed to have the dust and grime of the road washed from their feet. There was no servant to do this. Jesus became a servant and did it for His disciples.

We do not need to practice the same act of foot washing today. We do need to show the same practice of meekness and humility. We may make an apology to a Christian whom we have wounded, or we may take a meal to a home in a time of sickness. This is a modern sample of washing feet.

We do not need to feel that all the commands of the Old Testament are binding on us today. For example, the ritual commands of the Old Testament about offering sacrifices (Lev. 1—7) and eating certain foods (Lev. 11) are not spiritually important today. Jesus Himself is our ultimate sacrifice (Heb. 10:14). He declared that there was not a difference between clean and unclean foods (Mark 7:19).

The moral commands of the Old Testament are still in God's plan for today. The Old Testament forbids such pagan practices as fornication, adultery, homosexuality, and incest (Lev. 18:1-30). The Ten Commandments in Exodus 20 also are based on God's moral nature. We are to obey them today.

When we find a command or practice in the Bible which is confusing today, we must try to learn what principle the practice is showing. We often can show the principle with a change of action. We must continue to obey the moral commands of the Bible. They apply today.

WEEK 3, DAY 5

THIS UNIT: *Two Rules to Guide Bible Study*
THIS TOPIC: *Rule 2—Use Correct Principles for Applying the Bible*
TODAY: *Use the Bible Wisely*

Read Matthew 5:29-30,38-40; 18:21-22.

Sometimes the Bible writers used overstatement to make their points. You will make a serious mistake in applying the Bible if you don't recognize that some statements of the Bible contain overstatement. Some of the commands of the Bible appear foolish unless you see them as intentional overstatement or hyperbole.

In Matthew 5:29-30 Jesus urged His followers to tear out their eyes and cut off their hands rather than let these parts of the body lead them into sin. Did Jesus mean this literally? Absolutely not! He used hyperbole, exaggeration for effect. In Matthew 5:27-28 Jesus had warned against committing adultery by using the eyes. Then He talked about removing the eyes as a source of temptation. He does not want you to cut out your eyes. He does want you to fight against temptation with the same zeal that would lead you to remove the eyes. Jesus wants us to use mighty efforts to oppose all sin and evil. He used this figure of speech to drive His point home.

Another example of hyperbole is found in Matthew 5:38-42. Jesus referred to the old proverb of an eye for an eye and a tooth for a tooth. This principle originally had a merciful purpose. If a blow to the mouth knocks out a tooth, the injured person will likely try to do worse than knock out a tooth of his attacker. He will break a bone or inflict a fatal wound. This statement of an eye for an eye was originally a limitation of revenge. An injured person could do no worse to his attacker than he had received.

Jesus' words banish all the spirit of revenge. The injured, toothless party is not to try to knock out his enemy's tooth. He is also to put aside any attitude of revenge. This is symbolized by turning the other cheek.

Suppose that a robber comes to your home and knocks you down with a blow to the head. Jesus is not suggesting that you get up, turn the other side of your head, and say, "Hit me again!" He urges you to put aside a spirit of trying to get even with him. It is the spirit of revenge which Jesus wants you to banish.

In Matthew 18:21-22 Peter asked Jesus the extent of forgiveness which we should give to someone who sins against us. Peter felt that seven acts of forgiveness would be sufficient. Perhaps Peter felt that after seven acts of forgiveness a punch to the nose of his opponent would be proper. Jesus urged Peter to practice unlimited forgiveness. The figure of seventy times seven is symbolic of unlimited forgiveness. It does not require a computer check to keep a record. It simply calls for an unlimited extension of a forgiving attitude.

Memorizing Matthew 18:21-22 can provide you guidance in practicing forgiveness with other people. You will find it printed as the second memory verse for this week.

You have completed the second unit or major division in your study. We are going to make it a practice to complete a review each time you complete a unit in your study. You should be able to fill in the thumb and first finger on the hand diagram that outlines the study. Do that now.

Now fill in the blanks in the following outline of the material you have studied up to this point.

    I. One _____ (which is a _____ _____)

40

II. Two _____ to _____

_____ _____

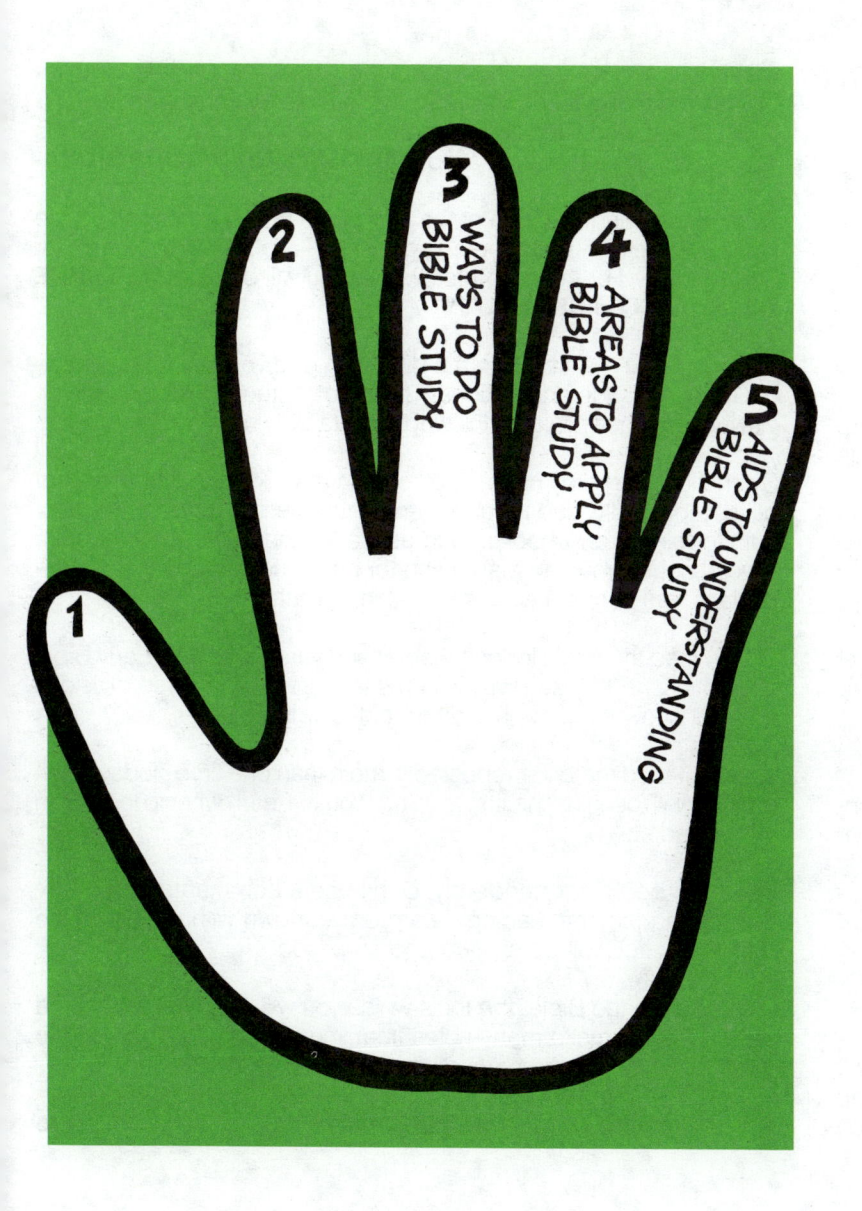

A. Rule 1—Use the right _____ for

_____ the Bible

1. Understand the writer's _____

2. Observe the _____

3. Accept the _____ of _____

4. Identify the _____ of _____

5. Use the Bible to _____ itself

B. Use correct _____ for

_____ the Bible

1. Apply the Bible according to its _____

_____

2. Use the Bible as a _____ of

_____

3. Use the _____ properly

4. Use a _____-_____

understanding

5. Use the Bible _____

41

WEEK 4, DAY 1

THIS UNIT: Three Ways to Do Bible Study
THIS TOPIC: Synthetic Bible Study
TODAY: Reading the Bible Continuously

Read Luke 1:1-4; Philemon.

What can you learn about a forest by flying over it? You can see how far the forest extends, how dense it is, and where the clearings are. What can you learn about a forest by walking through it? You can see the brooks, watch the animals, and trip over the roots. What can you learn about a forest by asking a forester? You can learn about its past, present, and future, and you can learn about its place in history. Each of these views of a forest corresponds to a way that we need to view the Bible.

We need a complete overview of a book of the Bible, and we get that overview by reading the book at a single sitting. This way of doing Bible study gives us the big picture of what is happening and is called **SYNTHETIC BIBLE STUDY.**

We also need a detailed view of the book. Here the words, sentences, and paragraphs become important. The prayers, commands, and promises of Scripture will have new meaning. We get this view of the Bible by slow, deliberate study with close observation. This way to study the Bible is called **ANALYTICAL BIBLE STUDY,** and it makes the detailed picture of what the Bible is saying become clear.

We also need to know the background and setting of a book of the Bible. Who wrote the book? Why was the book written? When was it written? What conditions surrounded the writing of the book? We can learn the history, geography, and culture that surrounded the writing of a book, and we can understand the political, economic, and social factors that influenced events in the Bible by consulting the writings of the experts and by making some personal observations. This way to study the Bible is called **BACKGROUND BIBLE STUDY.**

Look at the hand diagram at the end of the previous session to see what is written on the middle finger. That is your next unit or major area of study. For the next three weeks you will be studying **THREE WAYS TO DO BIBLE STUDY.**

Synthetic study of a book in the Bible can give you the broad picture of God's message and actions. This type of study looks for an overview without getting lost in a web of details.

Synthetic Bible study consists of reading a book in the Bible continuously, repeatedly, and independently. You must read the book without stopping. Long books such as Isaiah and Psalms may require several hours. You can read a shorter book such as Ephesians, Philippians, or Philemon in less than thirty minutes.

As you read the book, ignore chapter and verse divisions. Early Bible editors inserted these divisions. These chapter and verse divisions may not show the thought pattern of the writer.

You must read the book repeatedly, more than one time. Today, however, we will focus on the first reading. You will learn what to look for in a first reading.

Read the book independently. Don't use a commentary or study help during the first reading. Learn on your own with the aid of the Holy Spirit. You will be excited and surprised!

In addition to the Bible, the tools which you will need are a pen and paper. You will make many notes from your reading. You will add to these notes during every reading.

In your first reading determine the main theme of the book. Try to

learn the writer's purpose and goal. Here are some questions which you may ask as you read a book for the first time:
- Why did the author write this book? Did he state a reason? Can you determine a reason if the author didn't state one?
- How did the author carry out his purpose? What ideas did he present to support his purpose?
- What arrangement of material did the writer use? Did he arrange it according to time, place, or logic?
- What type of literature is in the book? Is it poetry, prophecy, narrative, an epistle, or a combination of all of these? See week 2, day 4 for further discussion of the types of literature.
- What is the emotional tone of the book? Does it express joy, concern, excitement, or an argument?
- To whom was the author writing? Was the book written for persecuted Christians, wavering believers, or those who are confused? Was it written to oppose sin, false teaching, or indifference?

Not all of these questions will apply to every book. Most of them will be useful in giving you some insight into the broad purpose of a writing.

If you read a book such as 1 Corinthians, you can observe much in the first reading. You can learn that the church was filled with people who were proud and ready to argue. They were practicing sexual immorality. There was also false teaching. They were interested in sensational spiritual gifts such as speaking in tongues and working miracles. They failed to love one another. They had not given generously. Many times in 1 Corinthians Paul used the phrase "now" or "now concerning" (1 Cor. 7:1; 8:1; 11:2; 12:1; 16:1). This seems to be Paul's signal to introduce a new topic for discussion.

If you read the Book of Romans or Ephesians, you will see a change of emphasis between Romans 11 and 12 and between Ephesians 3 and 4. In both books Paul spent the first chapters outlining important theological truths. In the later chapters he applied these truths in the lives of his readers. Both books contain the words "now" or "therefore" (Rom. 12:1 and Eph. 4:1). These words show that Paul is changing from one topic to another.

Did you note that your two reading assignments at the beginning of this session give an idea of what the entire books are about? Perhaps you should read those verses again with this in mind.

Now here is an assignment for you. Read the Book of Philemon at one sitting. As you do, look for answers to the six key questions that I have given you.

Your next Scripture memory assignment is Philippians 3:10. Do I need to remind you to begin working on it at once?

WEEK 4, DAY 2

THIS UNIT: *Three Ways to Do Bible Study*
THIS TOPIC: *Synthetic Bible Study*
TODAY: *Reading the Bible Repeatedly*

Your Reading Assignment Will Come Later.

You have learned to read the Bible independently at one sitting. You know that a continuous reading of the Bible gives you a sweeping picture of what the book contains. You have learned to look for the writer's purpose, content, and structure when you first read the book. Second, third, and fourth readings of a book help to uncover hidden treasures of meaning.

Read a book of the Bible in different versions. Such modern versions as the *New King James Version,* the *New International Version,* the *Good News Bible,* and the *New American Standard Bible* are useful for bringing out different ideas in their translations. *The Amplified Bible* may help you in learning the meaning of words. It is difficult to read quickly because it includes many synonyms in the text. *The Living Bible* is a paraphrase and not a translation. Many find this paraphrase helpful for comparison with another translation or for clarifying difficult language.

As you read a book for the second time, build on what you observed in your first reading. Observe more about the author's purpose and how he carried this out. Discover more about the time, place, and circumstances of the writer. Pick out words or phrases which frequently appear. Look for changes of mood or shifts in location. Notice a change in the topic of discussion. Rely on such connective words as *therefore, because, so that,* and *since.* Make a determined effort to improve your grasp of the facts about the book. Add what you observe to the notes which you made during the first reading.

In the second reading of a book make use of the paragraph divisions. Remember that these were added by humans and were not necessarily from God. They represent the opinion of a Bible editor on the thought divisions of a book. They can be useful to give us a means of dividing the thought of the writer into logical sections.

Look at Romans 12. This is in a teaching letter of Paul. The divisions of each paragraph are made on the basis of different topics discussed. Look at Genesis 12. This is in a narrative section of Genesis. The divisions of each paragraph show different geographical locations. The paragraph divisions of Revelation often show features of visions given to John by the Lord Jesus. The paragraph divisions of the Old Testament books of poetry such as Psalms or Proverbs are not useful for our study. The editors have indented each verse as a separate paragraph. However, most of the paragraph divisions which we will find give some help in providing a summary of the writer's thoughts.

Now I want to give you the Scripture reading assignment for this session. You are to read Philemon again; but this time you are to note, study, and analyze each paragraph. Identify the paragraphs in the version that you are reading. Then use the Paragraph Summary Form as a model to prepare a summary of each paragraph you identify. Use a separate sheet for each paragraph.

On a separate form for each paragraph, record the verse numbers for the paragraph. After doing this, use a sentence(s) or phrase(s) to summarize the content of the paragraph. After you have summarized each paragraph, you should look for connections between the paragraphs. Can you think of titles or themes for summarizing the content of the paragraphs?

Why don't you end this study session with a period of reflection. Think about the study you have been doing. Identify at least three things you have learned and three things that are different about your life because of this study. Pray thanking God for what this study is meaning to you.

PARAGRAPH SUMMARY FORM

Paragraph location _____

Summary _____

_____

_____

_____

Connections with other paragraphs ____

_____

Summarizing title or theme _____

_____

If you use the paragraphs from the *New American Standard Bible*, you will notice that the first three verses of Philemon are a greeting. In these verses we find the name of the writer, the recipient, and the greeting. In verses 4-7 Paul expresses a prayer. Follow through with a paragraph summary for the rest of Philemon.

WEEK 4, DAY 3

THIS UNIT: *Three Ways to Do Bible Study*
THIS TOPIC: *Synthetic Bible Study*
TODAY: *Making a Book Summary Chart*

Your Reading Assignment Will Come Later.

How many times should you read a book of the Bible? That depends on the book's length, your grasp of the material, and the amount of time which you have. Each time of reading should give more insight into the book. Each time that you read you will want to add additional observations to the notes which you have made about purpose, content, and structure. You will have further impressions about the content of paragraphs while you are reading.

At some point in your reading you will want to summarize what you have learned about the content of the book of the Bible. You can use a Book Summary Chart for this purpose.

A Book Summary Chart is a visual sketch on one or more pages of the content. Using a Book Summary Chart, like the one on this page, has three major advantages. First, it helps you summarize the key ideas found in a book of the Bible. Second, it helps you see the relationship between paragraphs in a chapter or a section of a book. Finally, it becomes a useful memory device to help you learn chapter and book content.

BOOK SUMMARY CHART
BOOK OF THE BIBLE _____

CHAPTER OR MAJOR DIVISION	TITLE OR THEME OF CHAPTER OR MAJOR DIVISION	SUMMARY OF KEY IDEAS OF PARAGRAPHS IN CHAPTER OR MAJOR DIVISION

Use the sample I have given you on the previous page as a pattern to make your Book Summary Chart. You will need to use a Bible with paragraph divisions. In addition, you will need blank paper, pen or pencil, and a ruler. The number of pages you need for your chart will depend on the length of the book of the Bible you are studying. For very short books, one page will be enough. For longer books, several pages will be needed.

Now, here is your reading assignment. You probably guessed it. Read Philemon again. This time, you are to prepare a Book Summary Chart by following the steps I will explain.

First, fill in the name of the book of the Bible, Philemon, at the top of the chart.

Next, list the chapters or major divisions in the left column down the page. A word of explanation may be needed here. In some cases, a major division of a book might include material that is found in more than one chapter. Remember, chapter and verse divisions were placed in your Bible by scholars to help in Bible study. They are not part of the original text. If you need to include material from more than one chapter when listing a major division, feel free to do so.

Now go to the next column, "Title or Theme of Chapter or Major Division." Write the title you would give to the material in the chapter or major division in this space.

Finally, write a brief summary of each paragraph in the chapter or major division. Write this in the wide column with the heading "Summary of Key Ideas of Paragraphs in Chapter or Major Division." Use the paragraph summaries you learned about in the previous lesson to help you make these summaries.

You can make an outline of the content of the book of the Bible after you have summarized the contents on the Book Summary Chart. Your organization of material on the Book Summary Chart can show the arrangement of the book at a glance. You can take the major divisions for an outline of a Bible book from your Book Summary Chart. These major divisions may reflect different times, places, or ideas. Beneath these major divisions you will place small divisions. These divisions may consist of chapters, individual paragraphs, or groups of paragraphs. You should write your outline on a blank sheet of paper. You may find some help in checking your own outline by comparing yours with another outline in a commentary or an introduction to a book of the Bible. Your outline does not need to match exactly what you see elsewhere. However, you will want to notice carefully if your outline has differed too greatly from what you find in other reference works.

It is important that you prepare this outline without depending on outside help until you are ready to check it. You will find great excitement in using God's help to discover what the Bible teaches. If you begin your study by relying too much on reference works, you will not develop your own creative style.

Let me remind you that in an earlier session, I stressed the importance of beginning to add to your personal library of Bible study resources. I am sure that by this point in your study you are realizing more and more the truth of what I said. I can promise you that in future weeks you will come to believe even more firmly in the importance of having Bible study resources at your disposal. I hope you have established a plan by which you can build a library of Bible study resources.

WEEK 4, DAY 4

THIS UNIT: *Three Ways to Do Bible Study*
THIS TOPIC: *Synthetic Bible Study*
TODAY: *A Synthetic Bible Study of Philippians*

Read Philippians.

Let's use what we have learned to complete a synthetic Bible study of Philippians. Our lessons for today and tomorrow will be long, but they are important. Completing these lessons can help you to master synthetic Bible study.

First, read the book independently at a single sitting. As you read the book, make your own observations. After reading, check the following list for some sample observations:
- Philippians is a teaching letter of Paul.
- Paul wrote the book from prison, probably from Rome. His comments in 1:13-14 suggest imprisonment, and his reference to "those of Caesar's household" in 4:22 points toward Rome.
- Paul shows several different moods throughout the book. In 1:3 he displays a thankful spirit. In 1:12-14 he shows a cheerful, accepting attitude despite his imprisonment. In 3:2-6 he shows passion and excitement as he opposes false teachers. In 3:12-14 he demonstrates spiritual intensity in his commitment to Christ. An outlook of joy appears in Philippians 4:4.
- Paul wrote this book to a group of Christian friends who had been considerate of him (4:14-16). There was some strife in the church (1:15; 2:1-4; 4:2), and there were false teachers to unsettle the Christians (3:2-6; 3:17-21).
- Paul wrote the book to inform his friends about his personal situation (1:12-14). He also wanted to encourage them to steadfast Christian living (1:27-28); to urge them to avoid strife (2:3-4); to introduce Timothy (2:19-24); to explain the plight of Epaphroditus (2:25-30); and to warn against false teachers (3:2-6). He specifically rebuked two women in the church (4:2-3) who were apparently quarreling.

In a second reading of Philippians try to summarize the paragraph content. Using the paragraph divisions of the *New American Standard Bible,* you can make these summaries of paragraphs in chapter 1:
- 1-2: Paul greets the Philippians.
- 3-11: Paul thanks God for the spiritual progress of the Philippians, declares his love for them, and prays that their love will grow.
- 12-26: Paul explains the results of his imprisonment and rejoices that some are preaching Christ. He believes that God will let him live in order to encourage them to live for Christ.
- 27-30: Paul urges them to endure persecution without being frightened.

You can complete your own paragraph summaries of Philippians. Then you will be ready to make a Book Summary Chart and an outline of Philippians. Indicate the major divisions of Philippians on your chart. Include also the chapter titles and paragraph titles. As a help in making your chart and outline of Philippians, here are some questions which can help you to see the major divisions of the book:

- What is Paul doing in 1:1-2?
- What is Paul's activity in 1:3-11?
- What subject is Paul discussing in 1:12-26?
- What are the spiritual needs among the Philippians which Paul discusses in 1:27 to 2:18?
- Whom does Paul commend in 2:19-30?
- In what areas does Paul give a warning in 3:1 to 4:1?
- What specific problems does Paul mention in 4:2-9?
- How does Paul conclude his letter in 4:10-23?

These questions can give you insight in finding major divisions of the book. Your divisions do not need to follow the same verse divisions as the questions, but the questions can serve as a guide for your study.

Philippians 3:10 should have seemed familiar to you when you read it. If it did not, you can be pretty sure that you are not keeping up with your Scripture memory assignments. Today you should begin your second memory assignment for this week—1 Peter 3:18.

WEEK 4, DAY 5

THIS UNIT: *Three Ways to Do Bible Study*
THIS TOPIC: *Synthetic Bible Study*
TODAY: *Synthetic Bible Study of 1 Peter*

Read 1 Peter.

Today we will complete a synthetic Bible study of 1 Peter. Our first step is to read the book at a single sitting without the help of study aids. Read the book and make mental notes about the content so that you can get a feel for the general flow of the book. Let me give you some clue questions to alert you to important ideas that will help you later.
- What kind of writing do you think this is?
- To whom is the letter written?
- What different moods do you see reflected in Peter's writing?
- In the middle chapters of the book Peter talked about how Christians should respond or behave in several different situations. What are these situations?
- Where do you think Peter was when he wrote this letter?

Stop and read now before going to the next paragraph. Then I will share my observations with you.

Here are my observations about 1 Peter. Compare them with the observations you made during your first reading.
- The letter of 1 Peter is a teaching letter.
- The readers of 1 Peter lived in the provinces of Pontus, Galatia, Cappadocia, Asia, and Bithynia. In New Testament times this was the northern part of Asia Minor.
- Peter also demonstrates varied moods throughout 1 Peter. In 1:3-4 he expresses praise to God. In 1:13; 2:1; 2:13; 2:18; 3:1; and many other passages he shows earnestness. His earnestness is mixed also with much compassion in 4:12 and with pastoral encouragement in 5:1-4.
- Peter wrote this book to a group of Christians who were facing painful suffering. The topic of suffering appears in every chapter of the book in such passages as: 1:6-9; 2:18-25; 3:13-22; 4:12-19; and 5:10-11. The presence of so many references to suffering provides an indication that this was the major theme of the book.
- In the middle chapters of the book Peter has placed some material which shows the response of a Christian in different situations. In 2:13-17 Peter talks about the Christian and government. In 2:18-25 he discusses slaves and their masters. In 3:1-7 Peter discusses the Christian home. In 3:8-12 he discusses Christians in their relations to one another.
- Peter probably wrote the letter from Rome. His reference to Babylon in 5:13 is probably a way of describing Rome. New Testament Rome was as wicked as ancient Babylon.

Do you remember the next step in completing a synthetic Bible study? Write that step here. If you cannot remember, review the materials for week 4, day 2.

Now you should complete paragraph summaries for 1 Peter. You should use the Paragraph Summary Form that I shared with you in the material for day 2 of this week. (There will be several chapters, so you should be sure that you have several sheets of paper before you begin.) Here is a sample of paragraph summaries from chapter 1, using NASB paragraph divisions:
- 1-2: Peter greets his readers.
- 3-12: Peter praises God for the living hope which he has and shows that the Holy Spirit revealed the plan of salvation to

Old Testament prophets.
- 13:21: Peter calls his readers to disciplined, holy living because of the high cost of their salvation.
- 22-25: Peter urges his readers to express their new life with brotherly love for one another.

Are you satisfied with your paragraph summaries? Remember, your paragraph summaries are YOURS. They do not have to be exactly like any other person's to be correct. However, it is important that you are satisfied that you have done a good job with the summaries before you go on to the next step, which is to **MAKE A BOOK SUMMARY CHART.**

Before you begin this step, you may want to review the material in day 3 for this week. You should use the chart that I shared with you in day 3 as you complete the chart and an outline. Show the major divisions of 1 Peter on your chart. Add also the chapter and paragraph titles. Here are some questions which will help you to see where the major divisions of the book might appear:
- Who performs the work mentioned in 1:1-2?
- For what is Peter thankful in 1:3-5? What is the effect of the trials in 1:6-9?
- What trait of character is Peter demanding from his readers in 1:13 to 2:3? Why is he demanding this trait? How are the readers to show this trait?
- What group is being described in 2:4-10? How are they to reflect their position?
- List the subjects which Peter is treating in 2:11 to 3:12. What groups would find these subjects a challenge?
- Who would be encouraged by the commands and promises in 3:13 to 4:19? What situation would these readers be facing?
- What group is addressed in Peter's final chapter? What encouragement does Peter give to their obedience?

Both this week's Scripture memory assignments have been from books you have been studying this week. Can you write them from memory?

Philippians 3:10

1 Peter 3:18

WEEK 5, DAY 1

THIS UNIT: *Three Ways to Do Bible Study*
THIS TOPIC: *Analytical Bible Study*
TODAY: *Making a Paraphrase*

Read Philippians 4:4-7.

Note that the unit you are studying now is about three ways to do Bible study. Last week you studied the first of those three ways, **SYNTHETIC BIBLE STUDY,** which gives you a broad, sweeping picture of a book of the Bible. Synthetic Bible study is a good method to use in beginning the study of a book.

However, you will not usually be teaching or studying whole books of the Bible at one time. Most often you will be working with one small section or passage at a time. The kind of study which can help you with a small passage is **ANALYTICAL BIBLE STUDY.** There are five elements in analytical Bible study. Note what they are in the Analytical Bible Study Arch illustration in the next column.

Each day you will study and practice using one of these elements. At the end of the week you should be able to draw the arch and label the elements. The element you will study today is **MAKING A PERSONAL PARAPHRASE.**

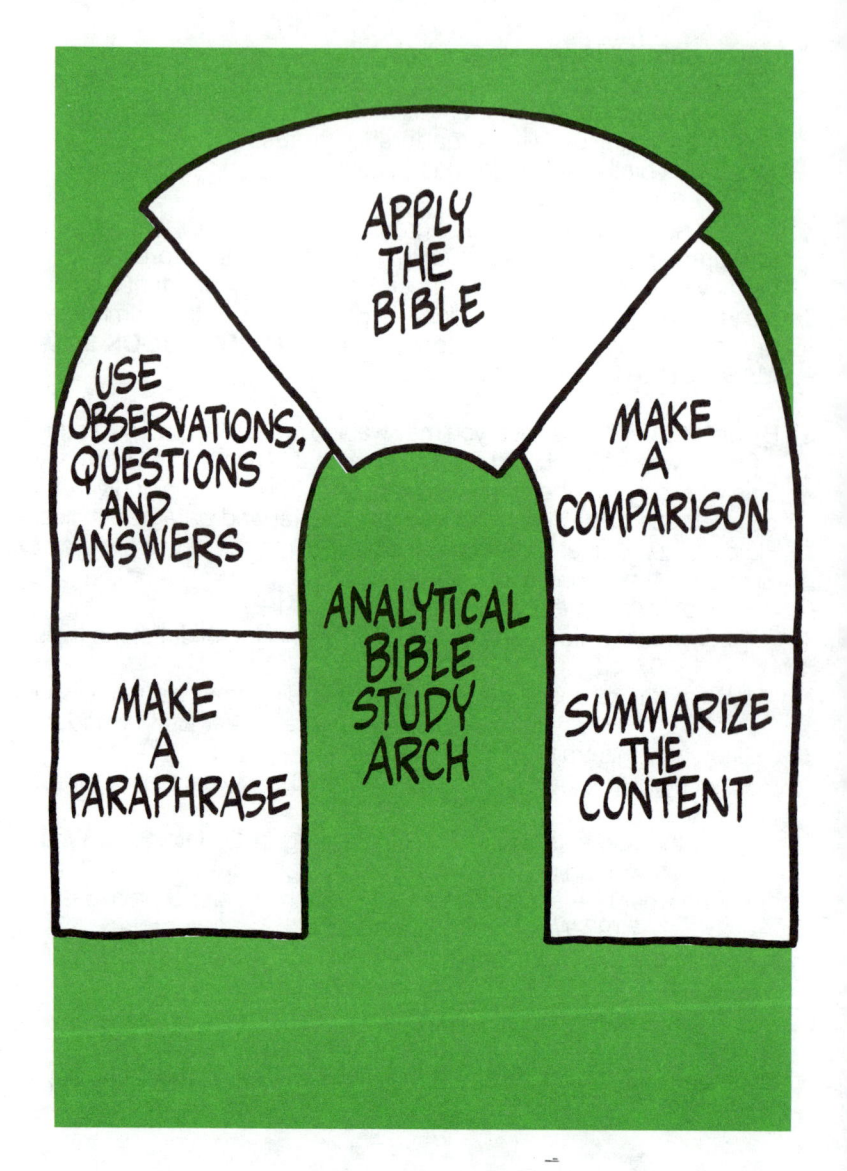

If you are going to study, teach, or speak on a passage of Scripture, it is best to use a paragraph of Scripture. The basic unit of thought is a paragraph. Sometimes you may be asked to teach or speak on a passage which is not a paragraph, but generally it is best to use a paragraph.

To make a paraphrase of a paragraph, read the section several times in different versions. As you read the paragraph, notice the main verbs of the sentences. Observe whether they are statements, exclamations, questions, or commands. Observe important nouns in the sentences. Settle in your mind what these words mean. Note carefully any words or phrases which modify the nouns. The modifiers will give you information which you can use in a paraphrase.

After several readings of a paragraph you are ready to make your own paraphrase. Take a blank sheet of paper and divide it into five columns of equal size. Place the word *Paraphrase* at the top of the left-hand column. You will use this sheet all week, so you should keep it with your Bible and other study materials.

Write out the verse in your own words. Do not copy the words of a modern translation or paraphrase. Try to write out the thoughts, attitudes, and purposes of the biblical writer as you understand them. Put the words in modern English. Keep your paraphrase in line with the teaching of the verses which you are rewriting. Sometimes you will use several words to say what a biblical writer has said in a few words.

The purpose of this paraphrase is to make you completely familiar with what the author is saying. It is a beginning of analytical study of the Bible. This paraphrase is the best way to make you aware of the ideas and thoughts of the biblical writer. It will help you to carry out the other parts of analytical study more accurately.

When you have finished making your paraphrase, you may check it again with a modern translation. You may learn that your paraphrase has brought out a different idea from the translations which you are using. If this is true, you may have given the verse the wrong meaning. You may revise your paraphrase after checking it with other translations.

HERE ARE SOME PROBLEMS YOU WILL HAVE TO DEAL WITH IN PARAPHRASING PHILIPPIANS 4:4-7

- NOTICE THAT THE VERBS IN VERSES 4-7 ARE COMMANDS EXCEPT FOR THE PROMISE IN VERSE 7. OBEYING THE COMMAND IN VERSE 6 IS A PREREQUISITE TO EXPERIENCING THE PROMISE IN VERSE 7.
- THE KING JAMES VERSION USES "MODERATION" IN VERSE 5. CAN YOU FIND A WORD THAT EXPRESSES THE THOUGHT MORE ACCURATELY?
- CAN YOU FIND THREE WORDS FOR PRAYER IN VERSE 6?
- HOW WOULD YOU DEFINE "GOD'S PEACE" AS IT IS USED IN VERSE 7?
- WHAT DID PAUL MEAN BY "HEART" AND "MIND" IN VERSE 7?

Your first Scripture memory assignment for this week is Philippians 4:4-5, a part of the passage you have paraphrased.

WEEK 5, DAY 2

THIS UNIT: *Three Ways to Do Bible Study*
THIS TOPIC: *Analytical Bible Study*
TODAY: *Using Observations, Questions and Answers*

Read Philippians 4:4-7.

Yesterday you paraphrased Philippians 4:4-7. Now you are ready to make observations and ask questions about the passage. On the worksheet you started yesterday, label the second column from the left *Observations and Questions*.

We can carry out the observation in two different ways. One way is to ask questions about the passage. For example, you might ask the question *who*. Who wrote this material? Who are the characters involved? For whom is the passage intended? Another question is *what*. What is happening in the text? What does it say to us? *Why* is another good question. Why did the writer say these things, and in what context were they written? *Wherefore* or *so what* may be the most important question of all. What difference does this passage make to people today?

As we ask questions about the Bible, we stimulate our thinking. We are forcing ourselves to take the Bible seriously. This will help us to apply its teachings more completely in our own lives.

Look back at Philippians 4:4-7. You are now ready to record observations and questions on this paragraph. Some of the questions listed can stimulate you to do your own study. What help would give you the meanings of the three words for prayer in verse 6? In verse 6 what practical activity does Paul challenge the Philippians to perform instead of worry? Why do we need to present the requests of verse 6 to God? Does He need the information? What is the relationship between verses 6 and 7? How would I learn the meaning of "the peace of God"? What does the word "guard" in verse 7 suggest about God's protection?

We also can use another set of observations to supplement the questions. We can observe:
- KEY WORDS: What do the verbs, nouns, adjectives, or adverbs mean?
- THE TYPE OF STATEMENT: It may be advice, warning, exclamation, or promise.
- CONTRASTS OR COMPARISONS: What is the writer comparing or contrasting?
- REPETITION: Are words or phrases repeated?
- QUESTIONS: Often a question in a passage introduces new ideas or summaries.
- CONNECTIVES: Look for words such as *but, if, therefore,* or *in order that*. What do they suggest about the meaning of the passage?
- GRAMMAR: Look at verb tenses and the use of pronouns, adjectives, and adverbs.
- ATMOSPHERE: What is the general tone of the passage?
- LITERARY FORM: Is it poetry, prophecy, narrative, an epistle, or a parable?
- GENERAL STRUCTURE: How are the ideas in the passage related to one another?

Often your observations will lead you to more questions rather than immediate answers. These questions will be of two basic types. You will ask questions about the meaning of certain terms, places, or statements in the Bible. You also will ask questions about the mean-

ing, significance, and application in life of what is in the Bible. List your questions along with your observations. Here are some ways to answer your questions about a passage:
- Use a dictionary to define unfamiliar words.
- Read different translations to obtain a meaning of a phrase or puzzling statement.
- Study other biblical passages which are cross-referenced in your study Bible.
- Think, study, meditate, and pray.
- Use a Bible study aid such as a book on Bible culture, history, or social life. Use a commentary on a passage only after you have struggled to arrive at your own answer.

You are near the midpoint of your study. Let's take time for a review of all your Scripture memorization. Note that each vertical and horizontal line in the puzzle is numbered. Each number refers you to one of your Scripture memory assignments in the list. One word in that assignment will fit the line of the puzzle and match letters with other words that cross it.

1. 1 Corinthians 2:14
2. Hebrews 4:16
3. Ephesians 4:32
4. Matthew 21:22
5. 1 Peter 5:7
6. Matthew 18:21-22
7. Philippians 3:10
8. 1 Peter 3:18
9. Philippians 4:4-5

Solution:
1. spiritually
2. throne
3. forgiven
4. believing
5. care
6. seventy
7. death
8. just
9. moderation

WEEK 5, DAY 3

THIS UNIT: *Three Ways to Do Bible Study*
THIS TOPIC: *Analytical Bible Study*
TODAY: *Summarizing the Content*

Read Philippians 4:4-7.

When you have finished your observations and questions from a passage of Scripture, you are ready to take your study a step further. A summary of what you have learned up to this point is helpful. Continue to use the sheet of paper divided into five columns. Label the third column from the left *Summary*. You are to base your summary on your paraphrase, observations, and questions.

The summary is an effort to help you clarify and summarize what you have learned about the passage. It prepares you to make application in your life or with others. You can use two methods in summarizing a passage.

First, you can state conclusions about what you have observed and questioned. The observations and questions are a beginning in studying a passage. They will help you to arrive at some conclusions about the meaning of a passage. In your summary you can state what you have learned about a passage. You are trying to say what the biblical writer meant as he spoke the words.

The conclusions which you will write will state the meaning of a passage and will evaluate its usefulness. This type of evaluation will help you to make a specific application of the passage in your own life in the last stage of analytical study of the Bible.

Here are some sample summary statements which you can write about Philippians 4:4-7. I want you to look at each one and evaluate

it before you decide on your summary. As you look at each one, ask: Does it summarize everything in the passage? Does it convey the feeling as well as the message of the content? Does it resonate with the way the passage makes me feel?

Now compose your summary of Philippians 4:4-7 and write it in the third column on your worksheet.

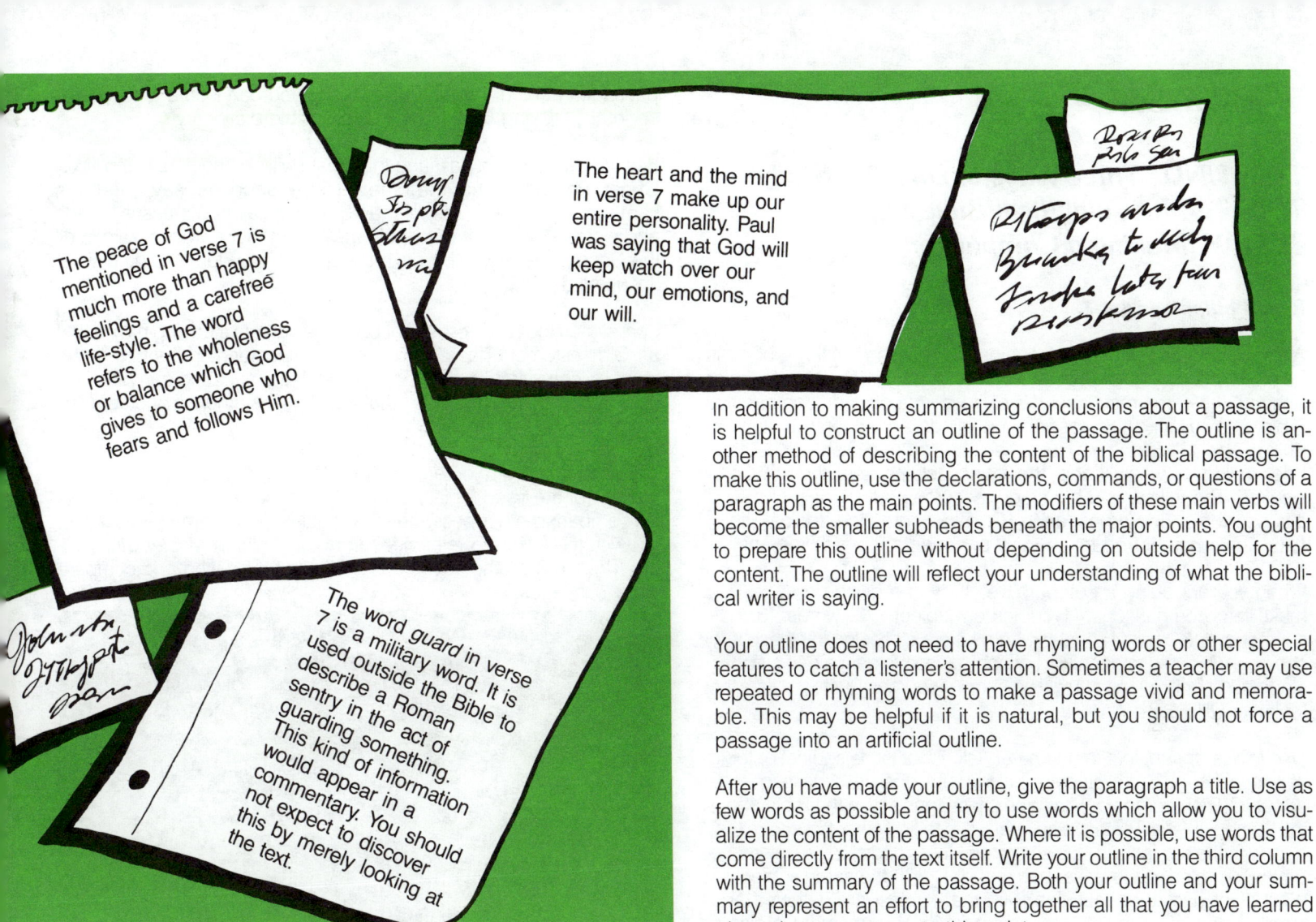

The peace of God mentioned in verse 7 is much more than happy feelings and a carefree life-style. The word refers to the wholeness or balance which God gives to someone who fears and follows Him.

The heart and the mind in verse 7 make up our entire personality. Paul was saying that God will keep watch over our mind, our emotions, and our will.

The word *guard* in verse 7 is a military word. It is used outside the Bible to describe a Roman sentry in the act of guarding something. This kind of information would appear in a commentary. You should not expect to discover this by merely looking at the text.

In addition to making summarizing conclusions about a passage, it is helpful to construct an outline of the passage. The outline is another method of describing the content of the biblical passage. To make this outline, use the declarations, commands, or questions of a paragraph as the main points. The modifiers of these main verbs will become the smaller subheads beneath the major points. You ought to prepare this outline without depending on outside help for the content. The outline will reflect your understanding of what the biblical writer is saying.

Your outline does not need to have rhyming words or other special features to catch a listener's attention. Sometimes a teacher may use repeated or rhyming words to make a passage vivid and memorable. This may be helpful if it is natural, but you should not force a passage into an artificial outline.

After you have made your outline, give the paragraph a title. Use as few words as possible and try to use words which allow you to visualize the content of the passage. Where it is possible, use words that come directly from the text itself. Write your outline in the third column with the summary of the passage. Both your outline and your summary represent an effort to bring together all that you have learned about the passage up to this point.

WEEK 5, DAY 4

THIS UNIT: *Three Ways to Do Bible Study*
THIS TOPIC: *Analytical Bible Study*
TODAY: *Making a Comparison*

Read Philippians 4:4-7.

After you have decided the meaning of a passage of the Bible, it is helpful to compare that passage with other passages which teach or illustrate the same message. We call this type of study comparative Bible study. During this session you will do a comparative study of Philippians 4:4-7, and you will need the same worksheet you have been using all week. Label the fourth column from the left *Comparison*. The following Bible study resources will be helpful during this session: study or reference Bible, concordance, topical Bible, New Testament introduction, and commentary on Philippians.

When you are doing a comparative study of a given passage, you make four comparisons: (1) topics or subjects, (2) words, (3) persons or events, and (4) context. Let's take a closer look at these and see how we can use each kind of comparison to gain a better understanding of Philippians 4:4-7. The study resources I just listed are the tools we will use.

Use topics or subjects to compare. Ask, What is the subject or topic of this passage I am studying, and what does this passage say about it? Then compare what other passages say in the Bible about the same subject. There are several ways to find other passages that deal with the subject you are studying. Most good study or reference Bibles will refer you to passages that deal with the same subject. A number of passages that deal with that subject are gathered and listed under that subject in a topical Bible. Your memory is also a valuable resource because you will recall having studied related passages at other times. Occasionally, you can locate related passages by looking up the subject in a Bible dictionary.

If you are studying a passage that deals with an incident in the life of Christ, compare what the other Gospel accounts say about the same incident. One Gospel may give a detail about Jesus' deeds and words that another Gospel omits. Comparing what is said in all the Gospels helps you have a more complete understanding of what Jesus said and did.

Sometimes the New Testament passage you are studying may quote an Old Testament passage or refer to an incident in the Old Testament. A comparative study of the Old Testament text can help you understand better the reason that the New Testament author referred to the Old Testament.

In Philippians 4:4-7 you are studying the general subject of worry or anxiety (or the need for faith and confidence). Let's see how you can do comparing other passages that deal with the same subject. Begin with the following references from the Holman *Master Study Bible*. Then, using other resources available to you, find and compare other passages.

> 4 [a]Rejoice in the Lord always; again I will say, rejoice!
> 5 Let your forbearing *spirit* be known to all men. [a]The Lord is [1]near.
> 6 [a]Be anxious for nothing, but in everything by [b]prayer and supplication with thanksgiving let your requests be made known to God.
> 7 And [a]the peace of God, which surpasses all [1]comprehension, shall [b]guard your hearts and your [c]minds in [d]Christ Jesus.

Use words to compare. The resources I have already listed will help you compare words. But a good concordance is probably the best resource for finding other passages which have the same words as the passage which you are studying. A concordance is particularly helpful when you are comparing often-used words such as *prayer, joy, anger, Holy Spirit,* and so on. Now let's take the word *supplication* from the passage we are studying and compare the way the same word is used in other passages. Use the following excerpt from a concordance to get started. Then use other resources that are available to you.

> **SUNK** Ps. 38:2, Thine arrows have **s** deep
> **SUNRISE** Luke 1:78, the **S** from on high shall visit us
> **SUNSHINE** 2 Sam. 23:4, Through **s** after rain
> **SUPERIORITY** 1 Cor. 2:1, not come with **s** of speech
> **SUPPER** John 13:4, rose from **s** and laid aside
>   1 Cor. 11:20, not to eat the Lord's **S**
>   Rev. 19:9, marriage **s** of the Lamb
> **SUPPLANTS** Prov. 30:23, maidservant ... **s** her mistress
> **SUPPLICATION** Ex. 9:28, Make **s** to the LORD
>   Ps. 28:2, Hear the voice of my **s-s**
>   Dan. 9:3, seek *Him by* prayer and **s-s**
> **SUPPLY** Is. 3:1, **s** of bread ... **s** of water
> **SUPPORT** Matt. 10:10, worker is worthy of his **s**
>   Ex. 17:12; 2 Tim. 4:16
> **SURE**—*trust* Num. 32:23, be **s** your sin will find you out
>   Ps. 19:7, testimony of the LORD is **s**
>   Heb. 13:18, **s** that we have a good conscience
>   2 Pet. 1:19, prophetic word made more **s**
> **SURELY** Gen. 2:17, eat from it you shall **s** die
>   Gen. 28:16, **S** the LORD is in this place
>   Deut. 14:22, **s** tithe all the produce
>   Ps. 23:6, **S** goodness and lovingkindness
>   Is. 53:4, **S** our griefs He ... bore
>   Mark 14:70 **S** you are *one* of them
>   Heb. 6:14, **s** BLESS YOU ... **s** MULTIPLY YOU
>   Ex. 31:13; 2 Sam. 17:11; Job 35:13; Jer. 23:39
> **SURFACE** Gen. 1:2; 7:18; Job 38:30
> **SURMISE** Acts 27:27, sailors *began to* **s**
> **SURPASS** 2 Chr. 9:6, You **s** the report I heard

Here is a hint that will be helpful when you are comparing words or topics. In addition to looking up the word or topic that you are studying, also look up synonyms (words or topics that mean the same) and antonyms (words or topics that are the opposite).

Use persons and events to compare. Often your study will reveal persons or events who illustrate the importance of practicing a truth you are studying. At other times you will discover a passage that highlights a person who ignored the truth which you are studying. This kind of comparison helps you to realize the way those concepts have worked out in human experience.

Think of some person who practiced, or some event that illustrated, one of the concepts in Philippians 4:4-7. Use a concordance or a Bible dictionary to locate and read about that person or event in the Bible.

Use the context to compare. When you do a comparative study of the Bible, you must be careful to observe the context of the passage. If you ignore the context, you may make a serious error in the interpretation of your passage. A good study or reference Bible, a concordance, or New Testament and Old Testament introductions will give you the context of the passage you are studying.

Use some resource available to you and discover the context in which Paul wrote Philippians.

After you have completed your study, list verses and important comments in the column you have labeled *Comparison.*

Today you should begin your second Scripture memory assignment for this week, and by this time it should be an easy assignment to complete. Memorize Philippians 4:6-7.

WEEK 5, DAY 5

THIS UNIT: *Three Ways to Do Bible Study*
THIS TOPIC: *Analytical Bible Study*
TODAY: *Applying the Bible*

Read Philippians 4:4-7.

Everything which we have done this week has brought us to the point of applying the Scripture. We have learned how to find the meaning of a passage. We have learned to evaluate what it is saying. We have tried to relate our passage to other passages which say the same thing. Now we will apply the passage to our needs or those of others.

You must base your application of a passage of Scripture on the meaning of the passage. Sometimes a passage of Scripture will give us a principle which we will apply in our lives. Sometimes our application of a principle will cause a different action from that which the Bible mentions. You will remember that the equivalent today of a "holy kiss" is a handshake. (See week 3, day 4.)

Be very careful in applying principles from the Bible to our own lifetime. Do you remember our discussion about eating meat offered to idols? (See week 3, day 2.) Paul decided to give up eating such meat if it offended another Christian. However, we should not give up all practices merely because they might offend others. Some Christians might feel that they should not share the gospel with someone lest they offend him. Sharing the gospel might be the very thing which would penetrate a stubborn shell of resistance. The principle is not that we should give up a practice just because we offend another person with it. The principle is that we should give up any unnecessary practice if it harms another Christian. Care and thoughtful use of the Bible can prevent errors in applying the Bible.

When we apply the Bible to ourselves, we must be personal, practical, and specific. We should write out an application for ourselves in a sentence with an "I," "me," or "my" in it. Our application must be practical. It must be something we can do, not something beyond our possibility. It also should be specific. If God has convicted us about prayerlessness, our application must include a specific plan to begin prayer.

We may apply the Bible to the needs of others or to our church. Here we must be careful not to apply the Bible to others without first using it on ourselves. Also, we will be cautious in announcing to others that we have applied the Bible to them. Much prayer should precede any effort to introduce the Bible into the life of someone else.

We will use some probing questions in trying to apply the Bible to ourselves. Among such questions are:
- What am I to believe? Is something in the passage about God, Jesus Christ, the Holy Spirit, grace, mercy, forgiveness, hope, or eternal life?
- What am I to do? Do I need to change some actions or confess some sins? Do I need to put away attitudes such as fear, worry, hate, resentment, or jealousy?
- What have I learned about relationships? Does this passage teach me a new truth about my relationship with God through Jesus Christ? Do I see new insights into my relationship with others in my family, community, congregation, or world?
- Is there a promise which I need to claim? Are there some conditions for my claiming this promise? Is there some word of encouragement or hope for me?

We must not use this list of questions in a mechanical way. It is an aid for searching out the possibilities of application. We are trying to find a command, promise, or example by which we can apply God's grace to our lives.

As you continue your study of Philippians 4:4-7, write your own applications under the last column. Label that column *Application*. Remember, these applications should be specific and personal.

This brings you to the end of your study of analytical Bible study. Do you recall that there are five elements in analytical Bible study and that I used an arch to introduce you to those aspects? Review your week's study by labeling the sections of the arch on this page. If you have difficulty recalling them, look back in the material you studied this week.

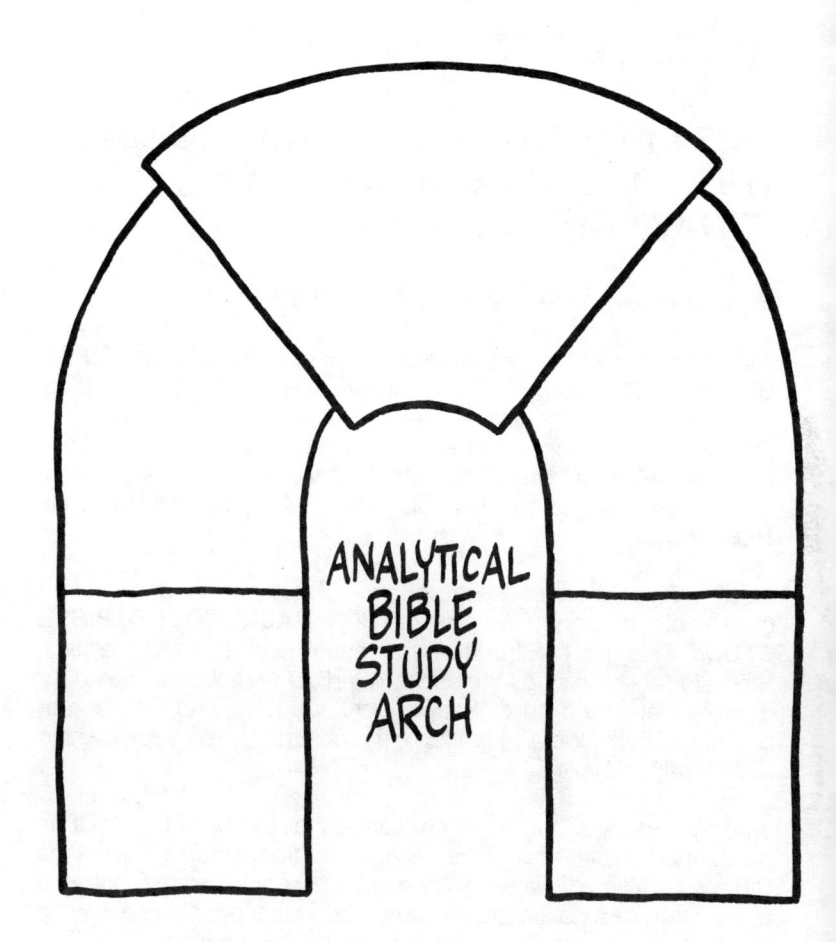

ANALYTICAL BIBLE STUDY ARCH

61

WEEK 6, DAY 1

THIS UNIT: *Three Ways to Do Bible Study*
THIS TOPIC: *Background Bible Study*
TODAY: *What to Look For*

Read Matthew 5:40; John 4; Acts 18:1-17.

Today you begin the third week of learning **THREE WAYS TO DO BIBLE STUDY.** First, you learned to synthesize a book in the Bible. You learned to see the different events and teachings of a book in the Bible and to put them together as a whole. We call this approach to study **SYNTHETIC BIBLE STUDY.** Last week you learned to analyze a passage. We call this approach to study **ANALYTICAL BIBLE STUDY.**

This week you will learn the importance of studying the background of a Bible passage. We will call this **BACKGROUND BIBLE STUDY.** This kind of Bible study can enrich synthetic and analytical Bible study. As we study the background of the Bible, we shall learn to investigate the history of an incident in a book and the geography of the Bible. We also will learn the culture and sociology which lie behind the Bible.

When we study history, we can learn either the background of an incident in a Bible book or the background from which a book of the Bible was written. If we study an event, we want to locate it in the life of a person or a nation. If we study a book of the Bible, we want to place it in the life of the writer or the history of a nation.

You probably know that Paul wrote 1 Corinthians. But can you place 1 Corinthians in the life of Paul? What do you know about his experience at Corinth? Acts 18:1-17 is a background study that will give you information to help place 1 Corinthians in the life of Paul.

> **READ ACTS 18:1-17 TO DISCOVER**
>
> Who were Paul's friends? What were they like?
> How did the Jews influence what Paul did in Corinth?
> How did the Roman government influence what Paul did in Corinth?
> How did God's leadership influence what Paul did in Corinth?

We will study geography also to learn the background of an event or a book in the Bible. We will learn the location of cities and the significance of bodies of water such as rivers, lakes, and seas. We will want to know distances between important points, prominent features such as mountains, and the general influence of geography.

Let's look at how an understanding of geography helps us understand the Bible or prompts us to further study. John 4:3-4 records: "He left Judea, and departed again into Galilee. And He had to pass through Samaria." The statement indicates that this is not the usual way that Jews traveled between Galilee and Judea. Look at a map of Palestine in your Bible or in a Bible atlas or look at the following sketch. What seems to be the logical, simplest, and most convenient and direct way of traveling between the two areas—route A or route B?

Are you surprised to know that nearly all Jews used route B? In doing the *unusual* thing, Jesus was actually selecting the most direct route. This means that all those who used route B were enduring an unnecessary inconvenience. Why? Do you see how an understanding of geography can prompt you to do further study? Since this is a familiar story, you know that the Jews selected the longer route to avoid passing through the territory of the Samaritans, whom they regarded with contempt.

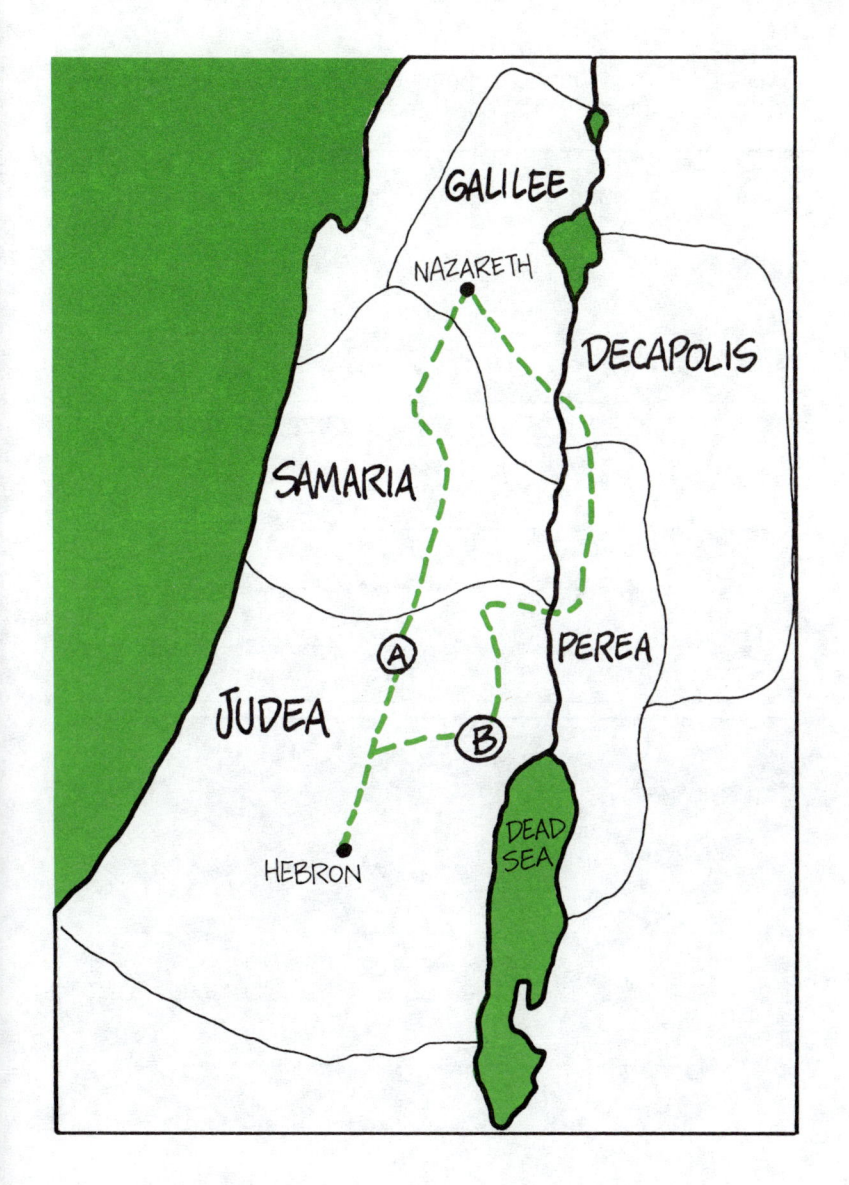

A study of geography can help us better understand Jesus' actions in John 4. Here Jesus traveled from Judea to Galilee by passing through Samaria. This route took Jesus into the territory where the multiracial Samaritans lived. Jesus made contact with many Samaritans and led many to believe in Him.

A knowledge of the culture of the people in the Bible will enrich interpretation. Culture involves a study of the intellectual interests in a civilization. It involves a knowledge of religion, science, music, art, literature, drama, and philosophy.

A background study of the Bible also involves a study of sociology. This is a study of group behavior and human relationships of all kinds. This kind of study can give us information about the family, towns and cities, government, travel, business, and social classes.

As we perform background studies with the Bible, we use two types of helps. First, we use the actual evidence from the Bible itself. Second, we use such tools as Bible dictionaries, encyclopedias, and various works dealing with history, geography, culture, and sociology. This is another reason why it is important to build your own library of Bible study resources.

Today you should begin memorizing Acts 17:11.

WEEK 6, DAY 2

THIS UNIT: *Three Ways to Do Bible Study*
THIS TOPIC: *Background Bible Study*
TODAY: *The Historical Background*

Read Acts 17:1-14.

The Bible writers wrote their messages in the middle of fast-breaking events of history. We will understand those books more completely if we understand the history which lies behind them.

Many helpful tools present the historical background of a Bible book or an event. The books of the Bible contain information about the history of the times. Often an incident in the Book of Acts gives helpful insights about events in Paul's life and ministry. Many incidental comments in books of both Testaments provide a wealth of detail about the historical background of a book.

In addition to using the Bible itself we will find that Bible dictionaries and encyclopedias give much assistance. Often, these tools call attention to items in the Bible which we would overlook.

Both the Bible dictionary and the encyclopedia contain information about people, places, and events listed alphabetically. Most church media libraries contain these study aids.

Let us look at the Book of 1 Thessalonians to learn something about the historical background of that book. We first want to find out something about the city of Thessalonica. We also want to learn about the history of Paul's relationship with the city and the church. We are interested in obtaining information about the time in which Paul wrote the Book of 1 Thessalonians.

Use a Bible dictionary or an encyclopedia to learn the following background information about Thessalonica.

Thessalonica was the capitol of what Roman province?

_____

_____

Why was Thessalonica an important city in its day?

_____

_____

_____

_____

What kind of relationship did Thessalonica have with the Roman emperor?

_____

_____

_____

_____

_____

_____

Now study Acts 17:1-11 to discover information that will help you to understand Paul's relationship with Thessalonica.

> How did Paul begin his ministry there?
>
> _____
>
> _____
>
> _____

> Who responded to Paul in Thessalonica?
>
> _____
>
> _____
>
> _____

> How did the Jews respond to Paul?
>
> _____
>
> _____
>
> _____

> Where did Paul go when he left Thessalonica?
>
> _____

To obtain information about the time of the writing of 1 Thessalonians, you should read those parts of Acts immediately before, after, and including Acts 17. Read in a Bible encyclopedia or dictionary the article "Thessalonians, First Epistle to." In Acts you learn that the events of Acts 17 took place during what we call Paul's second missionary journey. Paul had visited Philippi before coming to Thessalonica, and he went to Berea, Athens, and Corinth after leaving the city. Most Bible dictionaries and encyclopedias indicate that Paul made this journey sometime during the years from AD 50-53. They help you to realize that Paul probably wrote the Letter of 1 Thessalonians after the return of Timothy from Thessalonica to Corinth (1 Thess. 3:6; Acts 18:5). This is frequently dated around AD 51.

Here a combination of reading the Bible and using tools for Bible study provides additional insight into the historical background of this book. Did you recognize Acts 17:11 as your current Scripture memory assignment? You have until tomorrow to finish memorizing this verse, which is Paul's praise for the spiritual zeal of the Berean church.

WEEK 6, DAY 3

THIS UNIT: *Three Ways to Do Bible Study*
THIS TOPIC: *Background Bible Study*
TODAY: *The Geographical Background*

Read Genesis 11:31 to 12:5; Acts 13:1-13.

Biblical geography involves the study of the land in which the biblical events occurred. From a study of geography we learn information about cities, lakes, seas, rivers, mountains, and how these geographical conditions affected people.

The use of geographical information in biblical study makes the events of the Bible more vivid. A knowledge of geography helps the student understand and interpret the Bible more accurately.

Generally the Bible does not provide help for a person who needs to learn its geography. The writers of the Bible usually assumed that a reader understood the geographical features which were important in interpretation. Bible dictionaries and encyclopedias provide aid by giving information on the geographical background of events recorded in the Bible. A city, a river, or a significant geographical feature mentioned by name in the Bible appears under that name in these tools for study.

In addition, a Bible atlas provides much help in Bible study. Its maps assist in the location of unfamiliar cities. It also gives information about the distances between biblical locations.

The rapidly developing science of biblical archaeology provides assistance in describing life in the times of the Bible. Archaeologists have excavated entire biblical cities such as Corinth. Much information about life during biblical times has thus become available. This archaeological information frequently appears in Bible dictionaries and encyclopedias. It may also appear in Bible commentaries.

Whenever events in a biblical situation involve movement from one place to another, it is helpful to uncover information about the places and areas involved. This type of study leads to a better understanding of a passage of Scripture. After you have used study helps to obtain the information, it is useful to summarize the effect which the information has on the passage which you are studying.

In Acts 13:13 John Mark left Paul and Barnabas on the first missionary journey in Perga of Pamphylia. The Bible does not mention anything unusual about the geographical terrain around Perga. However, an article dealing with "Perga" in Bible dictionaries or encyclopedias indicates that Perga was a reasonably flat seaport where the disease of malaria was common. To stay in Perga could lead to illness. Inland from Perga the Taurus Mountains rose quickly to about thirty-six hundred feet at some points. This was a bandit-infested region and was dangerous and difficult for the traveler.

Why did John Mark leave Paul and Barnabas? The Bible does not state clearly, but it is possible that something about the unpleasant geographical features of the area may have had a part in his decision.

In Genesis 11:31 Abraham moved with his father Terah from Ur of the Chaldeans into the city of Haran. Abraham was living in Haran when he received God's call to leave for the Promised Land. Information about the city of Haran suggests that it was located on a prominent trade route between Babylonia and the Mediterranean Sea. In ancient times it was a center of idolatrous and pagan worship.

Now look at a map in your Bible, a Bible atlas, or the sketch included in this lesson. What does a knowledge of geography and of the customs of the time tell you about Abraham's journey from Haran to the Promised Land? Study the map and formulate your own ideas before you read further.

You probably discovered that Haran was located between three hundred and four hundred miles from Palestine. It would not be unusual today to travel that distance. In Abraham's day, it was highly unusual and would be equivalent to traveling many thousands of miles today. To have moved that distance is even more unusual. In Abraham's day, a man usually lived and died among his own people. What a display of faith it was to leave his people and to move to a land which he did not even know!

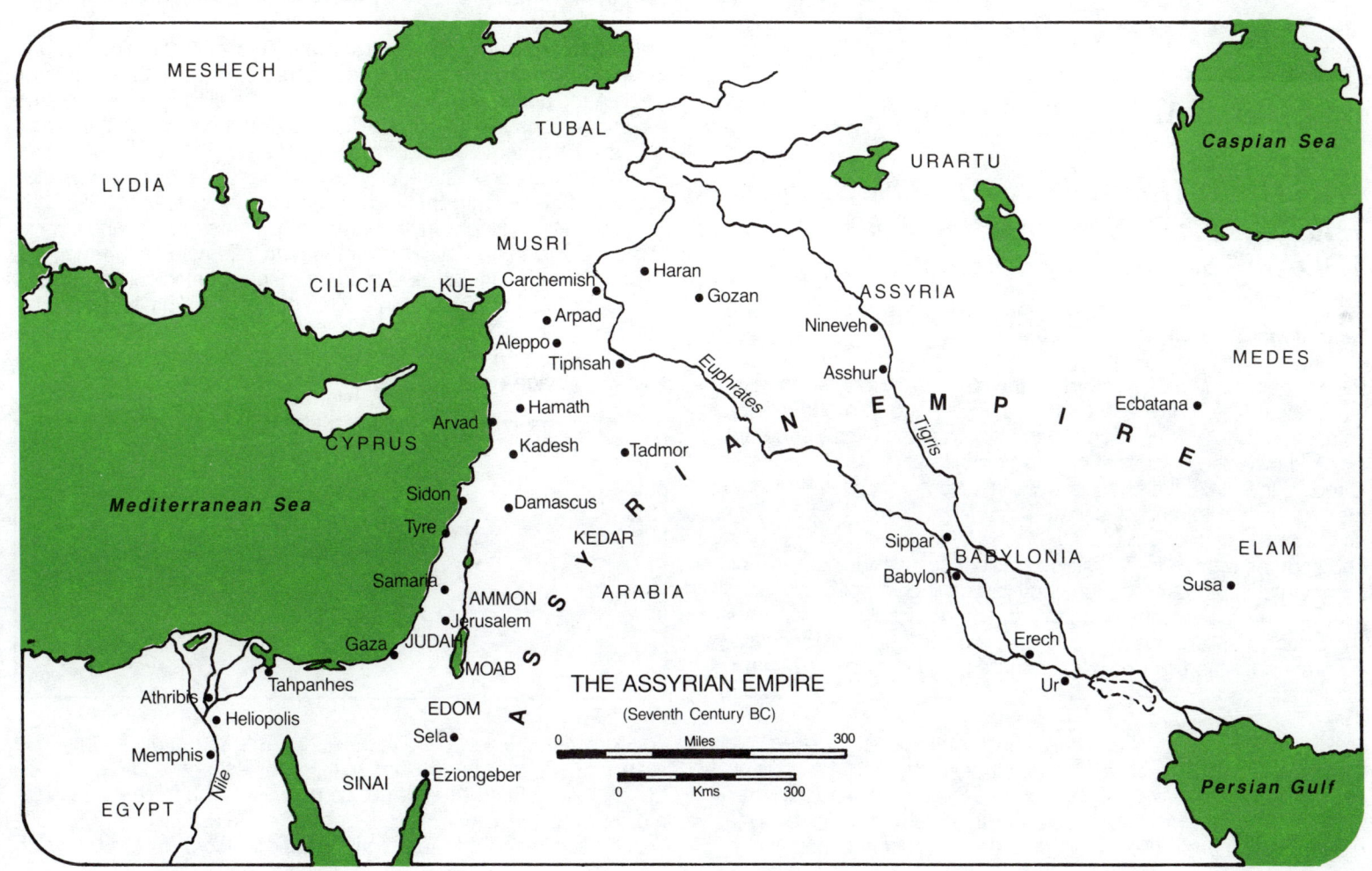

THE ASSYRIAN EMPIRE
(Seventh Century BC)

WEEK 6, DAY 4

THIS UNIT: *Three Ways to Do Bible Study*
THIS TOPIC: *Background Bible Study*
TODAY: *The Cultural Background*

Read John 2:13-25; Acts 17:16-34.

Biblical culture involves the study of the cultural environment in which the biblical writers lived. This area is broad and includes religion, science, literature, music, and many other areas of knowledge and art. A knowledge of biblical culture adds life and interest to understanding the Bible. It also assists you in making your interpretation of the Bible accurate and clear.

The sources of help for the study of Bible culture will include Bible commentaries. These helpful study aids will give specific cultural information on passages of Scripture. The previously mentioned Bible dictionaries and encyclopedias are other tools for discovering cultural information. These helps can be found in many church media libraries.

To illustrate the importance of culture in the interpretation of the Bible, look up information about almost any topic of the Bible which is unclear. For example, information about the Sadducees and the Pharisees would make many of Jesus' words about them clearer. What did they teach and believe? Why did Jesus denounce their hypocrisy so strongly? You can find information about these groups by looking under the proper article in a Bible dictionary or encyclopedia. After you have found the information, you will want to summarize how the information will aid in your interpretation of the Bible.

Let's try two examples of how a knowledge of culture makes our own Bible study more vivid and more accurate. In John 2:18 the Jews challenged Jesus to produce some evidence of His authority to drive the money changers from the Temple. His response to them was, "'Destroy this temple, and in three days I will raise it up.'" Jesus referred to His body as the *temple*. His hearers felt that He was referring to their beautiful Temple. The Jews' response to Jesus' words in verse 20 was: "'It took forty-six years to build this temple, and will You raise it up in three days?'" What was this Temple which they described? Study this passage in a commentary or look up "Temple of Herod" or "Herod's Temple" in a Bible dictionary or Bible encyclopedia. See what you can discover about the Temple the people thought Jesus was talking about. Do your study and write your ideas in the following space before you read further.

For centuries the Jews had a small, fortress-like temple for their use in worship. It was started under the Old Testament leader Zerubbabel (Ezra 3:8), but it was not as beautiful as the Temple of Solomon. Herod the Great, who reigned over Palestine from 37-4 BC, wanted to expand this Temple into a magnificent temple by which the Jews would remember him. He started his project around 20 BC, and the completion of the task required many years. The actual work had lasted for forty-six years at the time of the conversation between Jesus and the Jews.

The Jews were so devoted to this Temple that a threat against it seemed blasphemous to them. When the Jews felt that Jesus was threatening their Temple, they used it as a reason for encouraging His death (Matt. 27:40).

Another example of how understanding the culture can help us to better understand a Bible passage is Acts 17:18. This verse records that Paul preached the resurrection to some Epicurean and Stoic philosophers in Athens. What these groups believed had a definite influence on how they heard what Paul was saying. However, the Bible gives no indication of what those groups believed. Use a Bible dictionary or encyclopedia to discover this important information. Study and write your opinion in the box before reading further.

The Epicureans felt that a person ought to be satisfied with the simple pleasures of this life. These simple pleasures ought to bring a life of happiness and peace. The Stoics felt that a person ought to show courage and bravery in accepting the events of life. When Paul made his appeal to his audience in Acts 17:28, he used language that Stoics could understand. The Stoics were more prepared to accept the existence of a loving God who would meet their needs. The Epicureans felt that a person's future was limited to earth and depended on himself. Paul was trying to reach those Stoics who would listen.

Begin today memorizing your second Scripture memory assignment for the week: Matthew 1:23.

Stoics believed:

Epicureans believed:

WEEK 6, DAY 5

THIS UNIT: *Three Ways to Do Bible Study*
THIS TOPIC: *Background Bible Study*
TODAY: *The Sociological Background*

Read Matthew 1:18-25; Philemon.

Sociology is the study of all types of relationships among human beings. It includes the study of relationships in the family, communities, governments, business, race, and religion. Such tools as the Bible encyclopedia and the Bible dictionary provide sociological information.

To apply the sociological background of the Bible, you must find information on the particular institution or practice which the Bible is describing. After you have collected the information, you can summarize its effect and meaning for explaining the passage.

A study of the Book of Philemon shows some information about the practice of slavery in the first century and the attitude of the church toward it. Information about these practices appears in Bible dictionaries or encyclopedias under the article "Philemon, Epistle to." Also, most commentaries contain a lengthy discussion of slavery as it appeared in the New Testament world.

The Book of Philemon deals with the runaway slave Onesimus, who was owned by Philemon. An owner could brutally punish a runaway. Roman law suggested that whoever hosted a runaway was liable to pay the owner for each day of lost work time. When Paul told Philemon to charge to him anything which Onesimus owed, he may have been promising that he would repay Philemon for the time when Onesimus was a runaway (Philem. 18).

Slaves generally had no rights of their own. They were treated as property. Yet Paul asked for humane treatment for Onesimus and even dropped a hint that Philemon might free him (Philem. 21). Paul did not denounce slavery, but he established an attitude in the church in which slavery would slowly die out.

In Matthew 1:18-25 Joseph considered breaking his engagement to Mary when he learned that she was pregnant. In Jewish culture the breakup of an engaged couple involved something similar to divorce in our society. Joseph could have settled the divorce publicly with disgrace and potential punishment for Mary. He also could handle it privately by delivering to Mary a statement that he planned to divorce her. Joseph decided that he wanted to handle a divorce privately. While Joseph was considering the private divorce, an angel from God led him to consider completing the marriage. That was the course he followed.

During the engagement Joseph would have worked to accumulate a dowry to give to the father-in-law. This normally required about a year, depending on the wealth and income of the prospective groom. It was during this period that Joseph learned about Mary's pregnancy. His kind, merciful spirit led him to push away all consideration of divorcing Mary with a public procedure which could humiliate her. The second memory verse for this week is Matthew 1:23. This verse explains the fulfillment of the Old Testament promise of Jesus' virgin birth.

Information about the marriage practices which Mary and Joseph followed will appear in dictionaries and encyclopedias under articles such as "Marriage," "Mary," or "Joseph." Commentaries also will explain the reasons behind the actions of the couple.

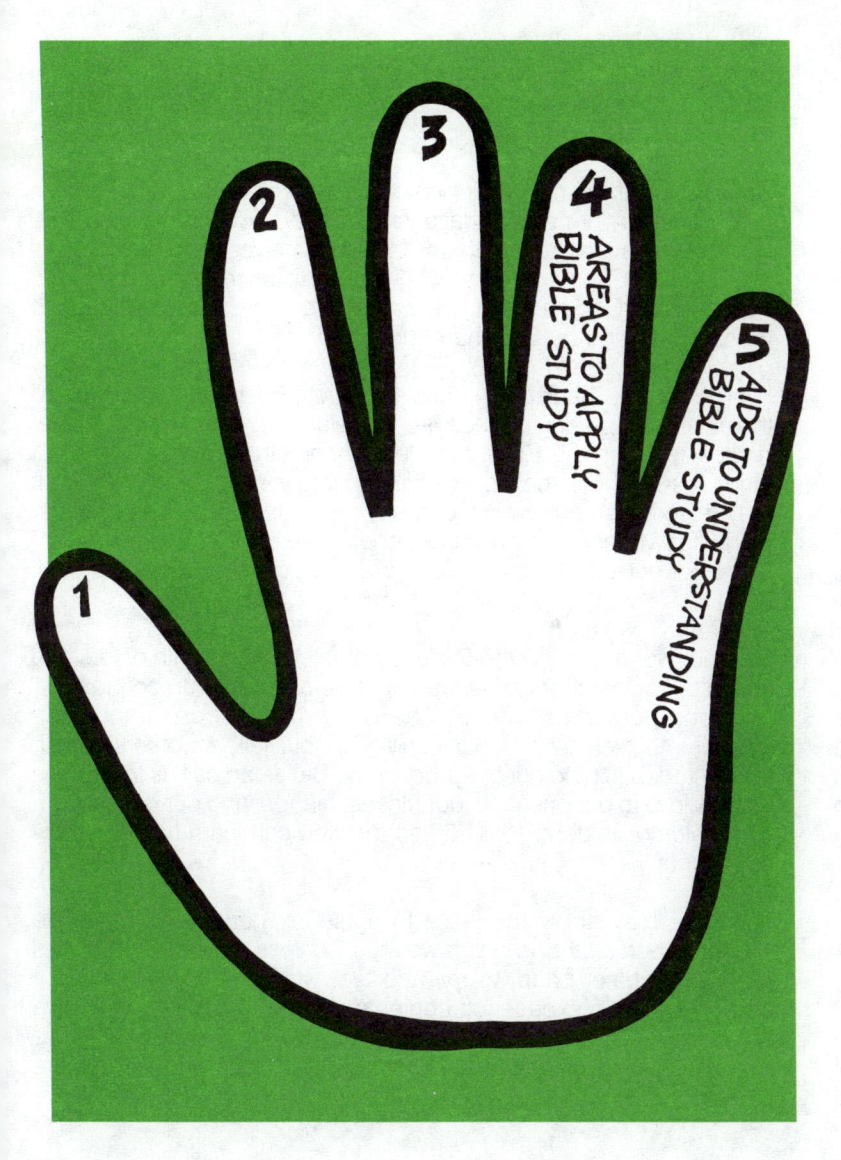

This brings you to the end of the third major unit in your study. That means it is time for another review. First, you should be able to fill in the thumb and the first two fingers on the hand diagram. See whether you can do that without looking back.

Now, let's add to our course outline. Look back to day 5 of week 3. You filled in points I and II of your outline at that time. Now, you are ready to add point III. Can you recall the key ideas and fill in the blanks?

III. Three ways to _____ Bible study

    A. _____ Bible study

    B. _____ Bible study

    C. _____ _____ study

If you had difficulty filling in the blanks, check the headings of the previous sessions in this unit.

Now review your two Scripture memory assignments for this week by writing them here.
Acts 17:11

Matthew 1:23

WEEK 7, DAY 1

THIS UNIT: *Four Areas to Apply Bible Study*
THIS TOPIC: *How to Apply Biographical Study*
TODAY: *Introduction*

Read John 13:34-35; Ephesians 4:11-16; Colossians 3:17; 1 John 1:7-9.

John 13:34-35 is your first memory assignment for this week. This will be one of the longer assignments, so you should begin memorizing it at this session.

Today you begin the fourth major area or unit of study. You can see at the top of this page what that area is. Look back at the hand diagram at the end of the previous session to see how it is related to the units that come before and after it.

The purpose of all study in the Scriptures is to lead us to apply it in our lives. You will want to review the five principles which we studied in week 3 on the application of Scripture. These principles will give you guidance as you explore the areas for applying God's Word in your life.

You may apply the Bible in many different situations of life. You must be certain, however, that you base your application on a right interpretation of God's message.

For example, John mentioned that Jesus "had to pass through Samaria" (John 4:4). John was not saying that God forced Jesus to go through Samaria. He meant Jesus chose to ignore the prejudice of the Jews toward the Samaritans and to take the most direct route from Judea to Galilee. The application to us is to conduct our life with an openness to chances for serving God. As Jesus passed through Samaria, He found such an opportunity with the woman at the well and used it for her application.

As we apply the Bible in our lives, we must look at four areas. One of these areas involves our relationship to God. Two of the others involve our relationship to others and to ourselves. The final area of application is to the church. We want to mold the church into the image which God has for it. We want it to express the love of God to those inside and outside the church.

First, we apply the Bible in our vertical relationship to God. We call this relationship vertical because we relate upward to God in obedience to Him. The Bible may tell us something to believe about God, Jesus Christ, the Holy Spirit, sin, forgiveness, or eternal life. It may describe something which we are to do for God such as choosing a life's vocation or making a special use of time. We must practice all of our beliefs and actions with a desire to glorify God (Col. 3:17).

Second, we may apply the Bible to our relationships with others. We call this horizontal because we relate across personal boundaries, from one person to another. The Bible may call us to show forgiveness to members of our families, to our fellow workers, to our fellow students, or to our neighbors. The Bible can call us to express Christ's love to our enemies, our closest friends, and our casual contacts. Memorize John 13:34-35 so that you can learn how we show others that we are Christ's servants.

Third, we may apply the Bible to ourselves personally. The Bible shows us personal sins which we must confess to God. It describes attitudes of hate, pride, worry, and fear which we must forsake. It challenges us to experience contentment, joy, obedience, and love as we live for God. As we confess our sins to God, we are able to live in a relationship of peace and harmony with Him and with others (1 John 1:7-9).

Finally, we apply the Bible to the church, God's people on earth. We want the church to demonstrate God's love, grace, and compassion for those who need to know Christ. In Ephesians 4:11-16 Paul describes the church as a fellowship where God's people find equipping for spiritual service. God wants the church to reflect His purity and holiness to others. As we read the Scriptures, we can apply its message to bring the church into this image and purpose.

As you read the Scriptures, try to apply its message in these four areas. The areas do overlap, for when we learn something about God, we often learn something about ourselves, our relationships to others, and the church. Learning these four possibilities of application can help us to be specific as we apply the Bible.

You are in for a double treat during the next two weeks of study. Our primary purpose is going to be to learn how to apply the Bible in four areas. List the areas in the next column.

1. _____
2. _____
3. _____
4. _____

The double treat is that you will be learning three more kinds of Bible study while you are learning how to apply the Bible.

Now let's do a brief exercise to introduce you to what you will be doing for the next two weeks. Pray about and meditate on John 13:34-35. Decide how you think this passage could be applied to the four areas. Then fill in the following chart.

HOW I CAN APPLY JOHN 13:34-45	
To my relationship with God	To myself
To others	To the church

WEEK 7, DAY 2

THIS UNIT: *Four Areas to Apply Bible Study*
THIS TOPIC: *How to Apply Biographical Study*
TODAY: *The Purpose and Principles of Biographical Bible Study*

Read Romans 15:4; 1 Corinthians 10:1-13.

One method of Bible study which encourages us to apply the Bible in our four areas is biographical study. This method of study looks at the lives of the people in the Bible. Biographical study of the Bible has much appeal because people are interested in the experiences of other people. The people of the Bible demonstrate actions which we can imitate and faults which we must avoid. We can look at one incident in the life of a Bible character, or we can survey his entire life.

The Scriptures indicate that God gave the stories of the Old Testament to serve as examples for us (1 Cor. 10:1-13). Paul reminds us that "whatever was written in earlier times was written for our instruction" (Rom. 15:4). The purpose of biographical study of the Bible is to learn the lessons which God has shown through His people in the past. There are numerous people, men and women, good and bad, whose lives we can examine in some detail.

The tools which you need for biographical study are: a Bible, a complete concordance, a Bible dictionary or encyclopedia, a pen, and paper. The general principle is to look up the references to the person in the Scripture. The Bible dictionary or encyclopedia will contain an article of information about the character whom you are studying. Reading the article will guide you in interpreting the information which you have collected. We will discuss this method more on our next day.

In this session I want to introduce you to four key principles of **BIOGRAPHICAL BIBLE STUDY.** Work through these slowly and be sure that you understand each one.

First, when you begin a biographical study of the Bible, begin with a simple and not a complex character. Some people of the Bible such as Barnabas or Priscilla and Aquila appear only a few times. Other characters such as Moses, David, and Paul are so important that you will not be able to master their lives quickly. Begin with a simple character and work up to a more complex character.

Second, watch for name changes and confusion of identity. The Bible contains the stories of several people with the names of Mary, James, and John. As you study these people, you will want to be sure that you are learning about the right character. Some people of the Bible are known by more than one name. Mark, the author of the second Gospel, is known as John, Mark, or Marcus, and many books will speak of him as John Mark. To gather all the facts about people mentioned with more than one name, you must learn the names which the Bible writers use for them. Usually a glance at a Bible dictionary, encyclopedia, or a concordance can give you this information.

Here is a quick assignment for you. Discover the number of times each of the following names appears in the Bible.

Mark _____ James _____
John _____ Zechariah _____

Now discover by what other names these persons were known.
Silas _____
Peter _____
Paul _____
Jacob _____

Third, realize that the experiences of some Bible characters will not always be found by searching for their names in a concordance. In the Books of 1 and 2 Timothy we can learn a lot about Timothy even in those sections where his name is not mentioned. Paul wrote both books to him. Information about Joshua appears throughout the entire Book of Joshua, even in those paragraphs in which Joshua's name may be absent.

Fourth, use your imagination vividly in biographical study. Learn about the customs and culture in which the person lived. Try to imagine how he felt and thought. Observe how he responded to circumstances. This will demand that you read repeatedly the Scriptures about the character and think about them.

As you study the character, do not look for outside help in understanding his life until you have thought about his life. Using a Bible dictionary or encyclopedia too early will rob you of the freshness and the joy of personal discovery.

WEEK 7, DAY 3

THIS UNIT: *Four Areas to Apply Bible Study*
THIS TOPIC: *How to Apply Biographical Study*
TODAY: *Doing a Biographical Study*

Read Every Passage That Deals with John Mark.

You are ready to learn how to carry out a biographical study of a Bible character. You will need to divide and label a sheet of paper as I have illustrated in the next column.

To do a biographical study, you should select a person whose strengths you admire and whose failures you want to avoid. Begin with a character whose life is simple enough to analyze easily.

After you have chosen the person for your biographical study, use a complete concordance to list all the references about that person. If it is at all possible, list every verse in which the name of the person appears. You may find information about that person's birth, growth, and death. You also may learn about a positive success or a miserable failure. After you have found the references in the Bible, learn all that you can about the history and life setting of the person. For example, if you study Barnabas, you may want to find out something about the missionary journey which he made with Paul (Acts 13—14). Later you may want to read some articles in a Bible encyclope-

```
┌─────────────────────────────────────────┐
│              PAGE 1                     │
│      BIOGRAPHICAL STUDY WORKSHEET       │
│   BIBLE CHARACTER _____ │
├──────────────────┬──────────────────────┤
│   References     │    Life Outline      │
│                  │                      │
│                  │                      │
│                  │                      │
│                  │                      │
├──────────────────┴──────────────────────┤
│                                         │
│              Summary                    │
│                                         │
│                                         │
│                                         │
└─────────────────────────────────────────┘
```

dia or dictionary about the events during the lifetime of your subject. For now try to use the Bible itself to learn all that you can learn about the person. Write down what you learn beneath the verse references which you have made.

List the observations which come to you about this person. Your observations may include questions or problems for which you want an answer. It may include positive or negative traits which you see in the person. Some of your questions may lead you to do more research later. You may write these observations, whether they are questions or positive comments, just under the specific Scripture reference to which they refer.

Now use the form you have prepared and begin a biographical study of John Mark by doing what I have outlined so far.
- Find and list each verse that refers to him.
- Study each verse or passage.
- Write beneath each verse reference what you learned from that passage about the person you are studying.
- With each verse reference, write any question or observation that passage prompts.

Are you satisfied that you have completed that much of your assignment as well as possible? Good! I want you to work on your own at this session. At the next session I will give you a chance to compare your work with some of the possibilities I see.

After you have collected information about the character you are studying, the next step is to outline as much of that person's life as you can. Sometimes you can see a chronological outline of the person's life. Sometimes your outline consists of the places in which he lived, a geographical outline. You may not have enough information to make this outline clearly, but an effort to use what you have will be helpful. Studying Paul's life, for example, becomes more meaningful when we divide his life into his three missionary journeys and his imprisonment. We can observe the changes and developments in each section of that person's life. Take time now to outline as much as you can of John Mark's life.

After you have organized the life of your character into an outline, look over your material again. This time identify some positive character traits of the individual or learn some failures to avoid. Among the items which you may want to observe are his general reputation, his aims and motives, his family and country background, his relationships and actions with other people, and his general personality and spiritual life. List these traits beneath your outline. You might want to use a separate piece of paper to list the traits.

After you have determined the positive or negative lessons from your biographical study, summarize briefly what you have learned from the person's life. Take time now to write a brief summary of what you have learned from your study of the life of John Mark.

There is one more step: applying the lesson you have learned. Next week you will learn how to apply this lesson to your relationship with God, to your own life, to your relationships with others, and to the church. Be sure that your application is specific and feasible. Make it something which you can do. Write down specific applications.

When you have completed the various applications from the life of the person whom you study, you may want to check your own study by comparing it with other helps. For example, if you study the life of Caleb in the Old Testament, check a Bible encyclopedia or dictionary for a good summary of his life. If your conclusions from personal study are that Caleb was a man of stamina and courage, you are on target. If your sources strongly suggest a trait which you have overlooked or question a trait which you have found, review your own interpretation.

WEEK 7, DAY 4

***THIS UNIT:** Four Areas to Apply Bible Study*
***THIS TOPIC:** How to Apply Biographical Study*
***TODAY:** Making the Application*

Read the Life of John Mark.

Today you should begin the second Scripture memory assignment for this week: Galatians 5:22-23.

Yesterday you found all the references to the life of John Mark which appear in the New Testament. You have written out the references and have made some preliminary observations about him, and you outlined as much of his life as possible. Now, as I promised you in the previous session, I want to point out some things so that you can check and possibly improve your work.

John Mark is mentioned as Mark in Acts 12:12; 12:25; 15:37; 15:39; Colossians 4:10; 2 Timothy 4:11; Philemon 24; and 1 Peter 5:13. He is mentioned as John in Acts 13:5 and 13:13, and the name John also appears in the previously mentioned Scriptures of Acts 12:12; 12:25; and 15:37.

As you reflected on these verses, did you observe that in Acts 12:12 Mark's family home was used in a prayer meeting for Peter's release from jail? Is Mark's father mentioned? What does this indicate about the influence of Mark's father on the son? What size home was probably needed to host the praying Christians? What does this show about the wealth of Mark's family?

In Acts 13:5 Mark left on Paul's first missionary journey. Mark is described as a *helper*. What does this indicate about the kind of role which Mark had?

In Acts 13:13 Mark left Paul and Barnabas for unexplained reasons. What does the terrain around the town of Perga suggest as possible reasons for leaving Paul and Barnabas? See week 6, day 3 for some answers to these questions.

In Acts 15:37-41 Paul and Barnabas disagreed over the question of taking Mark on the second missionary journey. What does the description of this discussion suggest about the intensity of their feelings? What happened to Paul and Silas after they began the second missionary journey?

Notice the gracious descriptions of Mark given by Paul in Philemon 24; Colossians 4:10; and 2 Timothy 4:11. In what area of ministry does Mark's most significant ability seem to lie? What do these verses indicate about Paul's willingness to indicate that he had made a mistake?

Notice the reference to the relationship between Barnabas and Mark in Colossians 4:10. What attitude does Barnabas show in his defense of and work with Mark?

Can you assign possible dates in Paul's ministry to the passages in Philemon 24; Colossians 4:10; and 2 Timothy 4:11? Are they Paul's earliest or latest opinions of Mark? What insight into the potential usefulness of Mark does the reference in 1 Peter 5:13 show?

Was it difficult or easy to develop an outline of Mark's life? No one certain outline is correct to the exclusion of all others. Compare your outline to the following one.
1. Mark's Home Background and Early Life—Acts 12:12
2. Mark's Opportunity for Service—Acts 12:25; 13:5
3. Mark's Failure—Acts 13:13; 15:37-39
4. Mark's Comeback—Colossians 4:10; Philemon 24; 2 Timothy 4:11; 1 Peter 5:13

What general traits of character did you observe in the life of John Mark? How did his early life affect him? What attitudes are reflected in Acts 13:13? What character traits appear in the later references to him in Colossians 4:10; Philemon 24; 2 Timothy 4:11; and 1 Peter 5:13?

Check your own evaluation of John Mark's character by surveying briefly an article about him from a Bible dictionary or encyclopedia. One fact which may come to your attention is that church tradition says that he was stump-fingered. This may mean that he lost a finger in an accident or was born without one.

Well, how did you do? Don't be disappointed or frustrated. If you had done a perfect job, there would be no point in your studying these sessions on biographical Bible study, would there? Take time to change or add to the work that you did at the previous session.

Now that you have observed characteristics in the life of John Mark, it is time for you to determine what application you can make. Remember, Bible study is always to be applied to life. God's Word comes alive when we let it speak to us in our daily living and relationships. Use the following sketch as a model to prepare side 2 of the worksheet you have been using to do this study. Then write in the different sections the applications you will try to make (1) to your relationship with God, (2) to your own life, (3) to others, and (4) to the church. Your statements should be clear, feasible, and specific.

HOW I CAN APPLY THIS STUDY	
To my relationship with God.	To my own life.
To others.	To the church.

83

WEEK 7, DAY 5

THIS UNIT: *Four Areas to Apply Bible Study*
THIS TOPIC: *How to Apply Character Trait Study*
TODAY: *Purpose and Principles of Character Trait Bible Study*

Read Galatians 5:19-23.

Today you will begin learning how to apply another kind of Bible study to your relationship with God, to your own life, to your relationships with others, and to the church. Let me help you learn how to do **CHARACTER TRAIT BIBLE STUDY.**

One of the aims in Christian living is to produce godly traits of character in our lives. Character trait Bible study attempts to identify the specific traits which the Bible commends and denounces. Then, we can apply the power of God to produce the positive traits and avoid the negative traits. Our ultimate goal in this Bible study is to become more and more like the Lord Jesus.

Character trait Bible study includes discovering what the Bible teaches about a particular trait. It has much in common with other types of Bible study such as biographical study and word study. It differs from biographical study in that we are studying traits or qualities rather than the entire life of a person.

The tools which you will need to carry out character trait Bible study include a Bible, a complete concordance, and a Bible dictionary or a word study book such as W. E. Vine's *Expository Dictionary of New Testament Words.* In addition, a topical Bible such as *Nave's Topical Bible* may prove helpful. An English dictionary will be valuable. Also, it is going to be necessary for you to understand the meaning of the following two words. Write the definition of each one. If you are not sure, use your dictionary.

A synonym is _____

_____

An antonym is _____

_____

As you carry out the character trait method of Bible study, here are some principles which you should remember.

First, study the character trait in which you have a vital interest. The trait may be one which you have but which you need to develop more fully. Don't focus on the trait because you are merely curious. Study a specific trait in which you have a vital interest for improvement. What are two character traits you would like to develop in your life?

_____

What is one negative character trait in your life that you would like to learn about so that you can deal with it more effectively?

_____

Second, concentrate on one quality at a time. Concentrating on one quality is like going hunting with a powerful rifle. With that rifle you can drill one shot into your prey in order to down him. Concentrating on many traits is like going hunting with a shotgun. You may spray the entire forest with buckshot, but you may not bag a single animal. When you focus on a single trait, you can take the time to make certain that this trait is built solidly into your life. If you had your choice, which character trait would you study first?

_____

Third, as you study this trait of character, study with the prayerful anticipation that God will produce its good features in you. Don't be disappointed if the trait is difficult to master. Fiery tempers and loose tongues do not develop overnight. Neither will a solution to these character deficiencies appear quickly. Focus on the specific trait which you need and continue with a prayer for and study of the trait until it is a part of your life. When you study the trait you selected as your first choice, what results do you expect that study to produce?

_____

_____

Fourth, as you struggle with character development, realize that some of the negative qualities in your life may be positive traits which are misused. An undisciplined waste of time actually may reflect a disposition to show such compassion to others that you forget about the clock. Is it possible that your negative trait you identified earlier is a positive trait misused? If so, how can you correct the misuse?

_____

_____

Fifth, recognize that some of the positive qualities in your life may be a reflection of a natural personality and may not show a deep spiritual conviction. A gentleness of outlook and disposition may come from a casual, lazy attitude which lacks initiative. The gentle spirit is good, but it needs to be based more specifically on a positive response to God.

Do not view character trait Bible study as merely an effort to master some facts of the Bible. View it as a means which God can use to produce in your life those traits which are pleasing to Him.

List here the Scripture references for this week's assignments. Then ask someone to use your Scripture memory cards to check your recall.

Assignment 1: _____

Assignment 2: _____

85

WEEK 8, DAY 1

***THIS UNIT:** Four Areas to Apply Bible Study*
***THIS TOPIC:** How to Apply Character Trait Study*
***TODAY:** Using Bible References to Study Character Traits*

Read Luke 8:15; Romans 5:3; 15:4; James 1:2-4.

James 1:2-4 is your first Scripture memory assignment for this week. Begin learning it today.

In this session you will practice doing a **CHARACTER TRAIT BIBLE STUDY,** and you will practice applying that study (1) to your relationship with God, (2) to your own personal life, (3) to others, and (4) to the church. Before you proceed, use a sheet of paper to prepare a worksheet. Divide and label one side as I have illustrated in the next column. Divide and label the other side as I showed you in week 7, day 4.

In a moment we are going to practice doing a study, but first let me outline the steps in doing the study. Here they are.

STEP 1
Identify the trait you want to study and write it at the top of the worksheet.

STEP 2
Find the meaning of the word in a dictionary and write it on the worksheet.

CHARACTER TRAIT BIBLE STUDY

Trait: _____

Synonyms: _____

Dictionary definition:

Antonyms: _____

Bible definition/teachings
(List references and summarize what each reference teaches.)

STEP 3
List synonyms that will help you understand the quality.

STEP 4
List antonyms of the quality. If you have a dictionary that gives antonyms, it can be very helpful. Some traits may have two or more opposites. For example, the opposite of joy could be sorrow. Or, it could be worry, self-pity, or even resentment.

STEP 5
Discover the Bible definition and teachings. Use a complete concordance or topical Bible to list passages in which the word appears. Study each passage and write a brief statement of what that passage says about the trait.

STEP 6
Reflect on your study. Use the following questions to guide your thinking.
- What are some benefits of this trait in my life and in the lives of others?
- What are some problems which this trait could produce in my life or in the lives of others?
- Is there a promise or warning from God about this trait?
- What factors cause this trait?
- What effect does this trait produce in the life of the church?
- Is this trait a part of God's character?

STEP 7
Write a brief summary of Bible teachings about this trait. Your summary may include information on how to produce or avoid this trait, as well as a statement from Scripture about this trait.

STEP 8
Identify ways you can apply the study (1) to your relationship with God, (2) to your own life, (3) to others, and (4) to the church.

Now use the worksheet you have prepared and the steps I have outlined to do a study of *patience* or *endurance*. The following observations will help you.

A dictionary will define *patience* as the state of bearing pain or trials without complaint. Other synonyms for the words are *steadfastness, perseverance,* or *stamina.* The opposite quality would include impatience, instability, or wavering.

The synonyms for *patience, perseverance,* and *endurance* are used several times in the New Testament. For example, in Luke 8:15 perseverance is used to describe those who hear the Word and bear fruit. In Romans 5:3 Paul speaks of tribulation bringing about perseverance. James 1:3 teaches "that the testing of your faith produces endurance." Finally, Romans 15:4 teaches that perseverance and the encouragement of the Scriptures bring hope to the believer's life.

What spiritual benefit does patience produce? How does this affect my attitude toward trials in life? What can happen in the life of a Christian who does not have patience? What are the means of producing patience in my life? Can I ever have too much of this trait? How does God show this trait? What will this trait cause in my relationship to myself? To others?

You should accompany each of these steps in the study of patience or endurance with a prayer that God will develop the trait in your life. As you study the trait, God can make its experience a reality in your relationship with Him, with others, and with yourself.

WEEK 8, DAY 2

THIS UNIT: *Four Areas to Apply Bible Study*
THIS TOPIC: *How to Apply Character Trait Study*
TODAY: *Using Bible Personalities to Study Character Traits*

Your Reading Assignment Will Come Later.

You already have learned to use Bible references to study traits of character. We found references in the Bible to certain character traits by the use of a concordance or a topical Bible. We learned to write briefly what each verse of Scripture states about the character trait. We also learned to look at many of these same passages and ask additional questions about the trait.

In addition to using specific Bible references to study character traits, we can examine the lives of Bible characters for these traits. This method of study is similar to biographical study, but it differs in that we primarily are studying the trait or characteristic.

All the suggestions which we have made about using Bible references to study character traits will apply when we use Bible characters to study those traits. We should study those traits in which we have a vital interest. We must concentrate on one quality at a time. We will pray that God will use the study to develop the trait in our lives.

The method of practicing the study will be identical to the method for using Bible references. First, we will select the quality which we want to study and find its definition in a dictionary. After we have listed a definition of the word, we also may list some synonyms and antonyms. After this beginning work, we will be ready to look for characters in the Bible who illustrate the trait that we are studying.

How will we find the names of Bible characters who show the trait we are studying? Sometimes we can draw from our general knowledge of the Bible. It really isn't as difficult as you may think. You would probably be surprised at the ease with which you can associate different Bible characters with specific character traits. Complete the following exercise to see how easy it actually is. Match the traits on the right with the characters on the left by placing the appropriate letter by each name.

___ 1. Job	a. love
___ 2. Achan	b. deceit
___ 3. Sapphira	c. encouragement
___ 4. Saul	d. devotion
___ 5. John	e. greed
___ 6. Ruth	f. wisdom
___ 7. Peter	g. patience
___ 8. Barnabas	h. benevolence
___ 9. Elijah	i. instability
___ 10. Solomon	j. forgiveness
___ 11. Hosea	k. courage
___ 12. Dorcas	l. jealousy

How did you do? We know that Peter's early Christian life showed the trait of instability and that John the Apostle was the apostle of love. This is how the traits should be matched with the Bible characters: 1-g; 2-e; 3-b; 4-l; 5-a; 6-d; 7-i; 8-c; 9-k; 10-f; 11-j; 12-h.

Sometimes we can use a concordance to find specific passages which talk about the trait we are studying. Often these passages will contain the name of a person who demonstrates those traits. When you search out passages about patience, you eventually will come to James 5:11 (KJV), which speaks of the "patience of Job." Sometimes a topical Bible will contain in its listings the example of persons who demonstrate the topic which it is presenting.

We can use a study of the life of Barnabas to develop the capacity for encouragement in our lives. To begin the study, we should define *encouragement* as including stimulation, consolation, cheering, or exhorting someone. The King James Version describes Barnabas as "the son of consolation" (Acts 4:36), and the *New American Standard Bible* translates the same verse as "Son of Encouragement." Depending on the Bible version which we use, we can use a concordance to study either the word *consolation* or *encouragement*.

Since Barnabas is clearly a person who gave encouragement to others, you could study his life to learn about encouraging other Christians. You will find reference to some encouraging actions of Barnabas in the following passages of Scripture: Acts 4:36; 9:27; and 11:23-26. You also will find several references to the actions of Barnabas on the first missionary journey of Paul in Acts 13—14. After Paul and Barnabas separated, Barnabas spent time with John Mark (Acts 15:36-39).

To use a Bible personality to do a character trait study, you should use the same steps that I outlined to you in the previous session. However, you should limit your consideration to evidences of that trait in the life of that character. When you have located and listed references to the trait in the life of that person, use the following questions to help you identify ways to apply what you learned about the trait (1) to your relationship with God, (2) to your own life, (3) to others, and (4) to the church.

- What is there in the life of this person that demonstrates the character trait I am studying?
- How did this character trait affect others?
- What final result did this character trait produce in this person's life and in the lives of others?

Now use the references I have suggested in the preceding paragraphs to do a study of the trait of encouragement in the life of Barnabas. Use the same worksheet model that I shared with you in the previous session.

Perhaps you can think of some other questions to use in studying the life of Barnabas in connection with encouragement. After reading the passages on the life of Barnabas, you can summarize what it teaches about encouragement.

WEEK 8, DAY 3

THIS UNIT: *Four Areas to Apply Bible Study*
THIS TOPIC: *How to Apply Devotional Bible Study*
TODAY: *Devotional Bible Study—Purpose and Practice*

Read Leviticus 11; Matthew 7:7; Mark 7:19; James 4:3; 1 John 5:14-15.

The unit or major division you are studying now is **FOUR AREAS TO APPLY BIBLE STUDY.** Those areas are G_____, your own L_____, O_____, and the C_____. If you have difficulty filling in the blanks, look back in the previous sessions for help. So far, you have used two different kinds of Bible study to make those applications. Those two kinds of Bible study are b_____ Bible study and c_____ t_____ Bible study.

Today you begin learning how to do **DEVOTIONAL BIBLE STUDY** and apply it to your relationship with God, to your life, to others, and to the church.

As we apply the Bible to our relationship with God, to our own lives, to our relationships with others, and to the church, we can use the devotional method of Bible study. This method of Bible study emphasizes the use of the Bible in changing our lives. Bible study can become dead and lifeless, unless we apply what we learn. The devotional method of Bible study calls us to make this emphasis.

Do you remember when we studied the analytical method of Bible study? If you have forgotten this, read again in week 5 to refresh yourself about this method. In analytical study we emphasized the importance of observing some of the facts and truths in the Bible, as well as the importance of applying the Bible in our lives. In devotional study of the Bible our primary emphasis is on the application of the Bible. We still have an interest in the facts and truths of a passage of Scripture, but our primary emphasis is on how the passage can change our lives. This method focuses on a spirit of eagerness to do God's will and to let the message of God change our lives.

As we practice devotional Bible study, we need to keep some guidelines in mind. First, we must always know exactly what the verse or chapter of the Bible means. If we don't understand what a passage is saying, our application can be horribly wrong. We already have seen how to interpret Paul's words in Ephesians 4:26 (week 3, day 1). He is not urging us to show anger based on petty feelings or wounded pride. Paul knows that righteous anger exists. He also knows that this kind of anger can change quickly into an anger which is selfish and uncontrolled. He is warning us against letting our righteous anger get out of control.

Second, we must evaluate the kind of passage which we are trying to apply. We must know whether a passage is talking about a truth which is timeless or temporary. Timeless truth is truth that applies to people of any time or circumstance.

We have learned to restrict the application of some Old Testament verses because their application has changed with information from the New Testament (week 3, day 4). The food restrictions of Leviticus 11 may contain helpful health information about eating. However, in Mark 7:19 Jesus declared that following those laws was not necessary in our spiritual lives. Also, some passages of the Bible describe a condition which we may not face in the twentieth century. However, the principle in the Bible that was used to face the condition in the first century is still valid in our century.

Third, we ought to relate the passage which we are studying to other passages which teach the same truth. When we do this, we can increase our understanding of the meaning in the passage which we are studying.

Jesus teaches about prayer in Matthew 7:7 in such a way as to suggest that those who keep on asking can expect God to answer their prayers. However, such passages as James 4:3 and 1 John 5:14-15 give other factors which we must consider in seeking answers to prayer. We will want to modify our understanding of Matthew 7:7 in the light of the teaching of such passages.

Finally, as we apply the Bible devotionally, we will want to reflect on the many areas in which a passage can be applied. We may learn a truth about God which we can apply in the political, economic, or social arena. We can find a truth about ourselves which can give us a higher call of commitment to God's will. We can uncover insights which will change our attitudes and relationships to fellow students, co-workers, neighbors, and even enemies. We can learn activities, goals, methods, and challenges which we can pray into reality in our church.

Now I want you to begin a devotional study of Ephesians 4:32, a verse you memorized earlier in your study. You will need to prepare a worksheet. Divide and label one side as I have illustrated here. Divide and label the back just as you did for the other worksheets I have shared with you.

DEVOTIONAL BIBLE STUDY OF _____

Summary of the meaning/teaching in the passage:

_____

_____

_____

_____

Is the teaching in this passage timeless or temporary?

_____

Related passages:

I want you to complete only the study steps on the front of the worksheet:
- Identify the passage to be studied.
- Summarize the meaning/teaching in the passage.
- Classify the passage (timeless or temporary).
- Identify, list, and study related Scripture passages.

As before, I want you to work on your own to complete this much of the assignment. At the next session I will help you evaluate this part, and I will help you complete your study by identifying ways to apply the study.

WEEK 8, DAY 4

***THIS UNIT:** Four Areas to Apply Bible Study*
***THIS TOPIC:** How to Apply Devotional Bible Study*
***TODAY:** Devotional Bible Study—Application*

Read Matthew 5:23-24; 18:15; Luke 23:34; Acts 7:60; Ephesians 4:32; Colossians 3:13.

At the end of the previous session I left you with the assignment to complete the first part of a devotional Bible study of Ephesians 4:32. At this session I will help you complete your study by identifying ways to apply it to (1) your relationship with God, (2) your own life, (3) your relationships with others, and (4) the church. But first, let me talk with you about your work on the first part of the study.

I hope you saw as you studied that you can use devotional Bible study as a part of your daily system of Bible reading. You also can use it in making a specific passage of Scripture come alive in your personal experience. When you do devotional Bible study, you always should be asking, "How can I use this Bible truth in my own life?"

There is no one certain way to word a summary or the main teaching of this passage. An interesting fact about devotional Bible study is that the summary of the passage and its teachings will reflect the needs that a person feels most deeply. I don't know what you wrote on your worksheet, but you probably dealt with questions like these:
- What happens if the person or persons I think I need to forgive do not want my forgiveness?
- Is my forgiving another person the same as God's forgiving that person?
- Does forgiving a person mean that I act as if that person had never wronged me?

Next, what did you decide about the timeliness of the passage? Is its truth temporary or timeless?

I imagine that you agree with me that the teaching in this passage is a timeless truth. It is easy to see that this passage contains a truth that Jesus intends for us to apply fully today.

The next step in your study was to identify related passages that you could compare with the passage you are studying. Some of the more prominent New Testament passages that deal with forgiveness are Matthew 5:23-24; 18:15; Luke 23:34; Acts 7:60; and Colossians 3:13.

Now let's complete the study by finding ways you can apply this passage. I want to suggest that you always do two things when you are identifying ways to apply devotional Bible study. First, pray that God will give you some insight about the application of the passage. Second, meditate on the passage. As you meditate, you should try to visualize or imagine how you might apply the passage. In this case, consider someone whom you need to forgive. What attitude must you overcome to offer this forgiveness? How can you express this forgiveness? In person? By a telephone call? With a letter? What can you do to demonstrate that your forgiveness is genuine?

Let me suggest a simple device that you can use to direct your meditation. There are five questions to ask yourself as you meditate, and these questions form the acrostic P-E-A-C-E. As you pray, ask yourself:

Is there any—

> **P**romise to claim or praise to offer God?
>
> **E**xample that I must follow or avoid?
>
> **A**ction or attitude to change?
>
> **C**ommand that I must obey?
>
> **E**rror that I must avoid?

After you have prayed and meditated on the possible applications, write on the back of your Devotional Bible Study Worksheet specific, practical ways this passage can be applied (1) to your relationship with God, (2) to your own life, (3) to your relationships with others, and (4) to the church.

Remember, be specific and practical. Merely saying, "I will be more forgiving" is not specific enough. Offering to express forgiveness to everyone who has ever sinned against you is not practical.

After you have written out the application which you intend, you should commit to memory the verse or verses which are a key in the study. You already have memorized Ephesians 4:32. This will give you a tool with which God can continually help you in the process of forgiving others. The challenge of forgiveness requires time for mastery, and continual help is essential.

Finally, you must put the application into practice. In the matter of forgiveness you may need to make visits, make phone calls, or write letters to express forgiveness to those who may have harmed or injured you. Avoid saying to someone, "If I've done anything wrong, I want to apologize." Mention specifically the item which demands forgiveness. Also, it is best if you admit negative thoughts about a person only to God. Mentioning the thoughts can cause another person always to wonder what you are thinking.

Today you should have memorized James 1:2-4. Begin memorizing Lamentations 3:22-23.

WEEK 8, DAY 5

THIS UNIT: *Four Areas to Apply Bible Study*
THIS TOPIC: *How to Apply Devotional Bible Study*
TODAY: *More Practice on Devotional Bible Study*

Read Lamentations 3:22-23; 1 Peter 4:19.

Today I want you to complete and to apply devotional Bible studies on the two passages you just read. You will need to prepare two worksheets before beginning. The following chart will give you some suggestions to help you in case you get bogged down. Other than that, you will be on your own this time.

	1 PETER 4:19	LAMENTATIONS 3:22-23
SUMMARY	Read 1 Peter 4:19 and summarize the meaning of the passage. As you do so, consider the type of suffering which Peter was describing. Was it suffering for one's faith, or was it the trials of life such as sickness, general discouragement, or loss of a job? Can the principles which Peter mentions apply in both of these situations? Ask yourself also: What does it mean to suffer according to the will of God? In what ways is God faithful? How has He shown this to me?	Read Lamentations 3:22-23 and summarize the meaning of the passage. Do a background study on this passage to learn such facts as who wrote it, when it was written, and how the writer came to speak as he did in these verses. A one-volume Bible commentary such as *The New Bible Commentary* or the *Wycliffe Bible Commentary* can provide some help.
CLASSIFY		Evaluate this passage for its present application. Since the writer is stating a truth about God, we can recognize that its content was true for the writer and for us.
RELATED SCRIP-TURES	Compare this passage with others which teach the same truth. Among those are the following: 2 Corinthians 4:16-18; James 1:2-5; and Psalm 73. Can you add others to this list?	Can you find other passages which teach a similar truth about God? Here are a few which you might investigate: Romans 8:28-31; Psalm 84:11; and Psalm 118:24.
APPLICATIONS	As you apply this passage to your own life, can you think of specific items which are causing you suffering? Can you visualize what might be involved in trusting yourself to God in this matter? Which of the words of the P-E-A-C-E acrostic is most applicable to you? Does this verse provide a promise, example, action or attitude, command, or error to be noted? Can you write a specific application of this verse? What is the primary area of application which you are making? Does it deal with your understanding of God, your understanding of yourself, your relationship to someone else, or your relationship to your church? Here are some considerations to assist you in the application of this passage. Most people respond to difficulty in life by showing self-pity, by becoming angry at God or someone else, or by losing all will to endure. Have you shown any of these responses? Recognize that all of us encounter daily hardships and difficulties in which we must have God's strength and presence. Don't respond to this passage by saying, "If I ever need this truth, I'll remember it." You already need God's strength and must apply it daily.	As you apply this passage to your own life, can you think of specific items which you often think about instead of God's mercies? Do these items cause you worry, fear, resentment, or depression? How could it help your problem if you reflected more on what God will do for you in His faithfulness and mercy? Which of the words of the P-E-A-C-E acrostic are most useful to you here? Do you find a promise, example, action or attitude, command, or error which you must observe? Can you find a specific application of this verse in your life? In what area of your life is it helpful? Does it change your idea of God, your understanding of yourself, your relationship to another person, or your attitude toward your church?

WEEK 9, DAY 1

THIS UNIT: *Five Aids to Understanding Bible Study*
THIS TOPIC: *Studying and Understanding Words*
TODAY: *How to Do a Word Study*

Read Ephesians 1:1-2; 1 Peter 2:9.

The first Scripture memory assignment for this week is Hebrews 12:14. Begin memorizing during this session.

The Bible most of us use is easy to read and understand. It has been translated into English. Many good English translations and paraphrases are available to us.

The authors of the Bible did not write in English. They wrote in the languages of Hebrew, Aramaic, and Greek. Because the words of these languages do not always have exact equivalents in English, a knowledge of the original languages is a great help in studying the Bible. Most of us, however, are not scholars. We must use our English Bible and the aids for Bible study that are available to us. We will discover more about these aids and their use in the studies that are yet to come. A good method of Bible study is doing word studies. The following guidelines will help you with this study method. Think about how following these guidelines can improve your Bible study. Identify the ones that already are a part of your Bible study habits. At the next session we will use these guidelines to do a word study.

GUIDELINE 1

Know whether the word you are studying is broad or narrow. A narrow word is a word which has a rather limited meaning and usage. To determine whether your word is broad or narrow, ask whether your word deals with a theme of the Bible which is large and prominent.

Now look at the two passages you read at the beginning of this session and select three words that would probably be more difficult to study because of their broad meanings.

_____   _____   _____

GUIDELINE 2

Try to discover the meanings of the words as they are used in the Bible. You do not have to be a scholar to do this. A Bible dictionary or a good reference Bible will help you understand Bible words. For example, the Holman *Master Study Bible* contains an encyclopedia that explains many Bible words. A complete concordance is another valuable tool for doing word studies. Most Bibles have a concordance, but these usually are limited to a few pages. *Harper's Topical Concordance* is a good Bible study aid. This book organizes material from the Bible around many topics. A student usually can find a lot of information about a Bible word in this volume. *Cruden's Complete Concordance* is another helpful tool. This book takes Bible words and gives references to their use.

The Bible student who wants to study in more depth can use a volume such as *Young's Analytical Concordance to the Bible*. This book indicates the Hebrew or Greek word that lies behind the word you are studying.

GUIDELINE 3
Be certain to observe the context in which a word appears. The context is always the best indicator of the proper meaning of a word. In English the word *saint* carries a special notion of holiness or pious living. In the New Testament the word for *saint* appears in the introductions to several of Paul's letters (Eph. 1:1; Phil. 1:1; Col. 1:2) and is a reference to all Christians in the church. Paul is not saying that all members of the church were perfect or pious in their living. Paul saw all Christians as set apart to do God's will. They were saints in this sense.

GUIDELINE 4
Don't let word study be the only method of Bible study which you use. By its nature this method focuses intensively on the small details of word meanings. Supplement your study of the words in the Bible with other methods of Bible study, such as the synthetic or historical method, so that you can gain a full picture of what God is saying.

As you probably anticipated, I want to give you a model for another worksheet. Use the following model to prepare a worksheet for your study session tomorrow. Prepare the front as I have illustrated. Prepare the back as you did for all the others.

WORD STUDY WORKSHEET

Word: _____

Dictionary definition including synonyms and antonyms:

Bible usages:

Bible meaning:

Summary:

WEEK 9, DAY 2

THIS UNIT: *Five Aids to Understanding Bible Study*
THIS TOPIC: *Studying and Understanding Words*
TODAY: *Practicing Word Study*

Your Reading Assignment Will Come Later.

Today I want to walk you through a six-step procedure for doing a word study and let you practice some of the steps. Take your time and be sure you understand each step because I am going to ask you to give them back to me at the end of the session. Here are the steps.

STEP 1
SELECT THE WORD TO STUDY

First, carefully select the word you want to study. Until you have developed your skills in doing a word study, you should not select a word with a broad meaning. Select a word with a meaning narrow enough to study easily.

STEP 2
DEFINE THE WORD

Look up and record the definition from an English dictionary. Be sure to include synonyms and antonyms. Let's imagine that you are doing a word study using the word *sanctification*. What is the dictionary definition? You may need to summarize the definition if it is long. What synonyms and antonyms can you think of?

SYNONYMS	ANTONYMS
_____	_____
_____	_____
_____	_____

STEP 3
DISCOVER BIBLE USAGES

Use a concordance to find and list passages in the Bible in which the word is used. Next, look up the word *sanctification* in the *Master Study Bible*. You will discover that the word is used in both the Old Testament and the New Testament. You will find also that the English words *consecrate*, *holy*, and *holiness* are sometimes used to translate the word that is usually translated *sanctification*.

If you have access to *Young's Analytical Concordance to the Bible* or another complete concordance, look up the word *sanctification*. You will find the words *sanctify* and *sanctified* as well. These words mean set apart, or separated to God.

You should write down the references of the verses in which the words *sanctification, sanctify, consecrate,* or *holy* appear. As you do this, you will want to observe the books in which the words appear, the writers who use the words, and the usage of the word in the text where they appear. Writing out what you observe can help you to retain the results of your study. Some of the comments which you might make about each verse would include the motivation toward sanctification, the means of obtaining sanctification, and a biblical definition of what is included in santification. Write three of the references you found and your comments about how the word is used.

_____

Modern English translations also help by giving you additional information about the meanings or shadings of meaning that the word may have. The word *holiness* appears in Romans 6:19 in the King James Version. Use at least two modern English translations to see what word is used instead of *holiness*.

STEP 4
IDENTIFY THE BIBLE MEANING
The next step is to write a definition that expresses the way the word is used in the Bible. Just for fun, before you read further, how would you define *sanctification* to explain how it is used in the Bible?

Looking up a word in *Young's Analytical Concordance to the Bible* is an excellent way to determine its Bible meaning. Check the definition you wrote against the one found in that concordance.

STEP 5
SUMMARIZE WHAT YOU HAVE LEARNED
Write a summary of what you have learned about the word you are studying. The summary may be an outline of biblical teachings about the word, or it may be an original paragraph that you compose. The important thing about the summary is that it opens the door for the applications you will plan in the next step.

STEP 6
PLAN APPLICATIONS
Use the back of the worksheet to plan applications just as you have in the other kinds of Bible study you have learned. By this time in the study, you should have developed a reasonable amount of skill in identifying and planning these applications.

There you have the six steps. Without looking back, see whether you can review the steps by listing them here.

At the next session you will have an opportunity to do a word study.

WEEK 9, DAY 3

THIS UNIT: *Five Aids to Understanding Bible Study*
THIS TOPIC: *Studying and Understanding Words*
TODAY: *A Practice Word Study*

Read Passages That Deal with the Word ANXIOUS.

The two previous sessions were to prepare you for the word study that I want you to do now. I am going to suggest six steps for you to follow. If you follow these steps carefully, you will have a good experience with this study.

Step 1—Select the word. The first step in doing a word study is obvious. You must decide what Bible word you want to study. I'm going to do that step for you by assigning you the word *anxious*. I think you have an interest in finding out what you can learn from studying this word in the Bible. This study would be spiritually helpful, and the word is narrow enough that you can follow it easily.

Use the worksheet that you prepared and work on your own to complete the study. After you have completed your work, read on, and I will compare notes with you.

> STOP AND WORK BEFORE READING ON

Now let's look at your work a step at a time. I want to call your attention to some checkpoints and compare notes with you at several places in the study. Remember, however, your study does not have to be a carbon copy of what I say. What you decide and the places you put the emphasis in your study reflect the needs you feel and the place you are in your spiritual growth. We will skip the first step because I assigned the word to you instead of giving you a choice.

Step 2—Define the word. I have made it a point to invest in a good dictionary as a part of my personal library of study resources. So, I had little difficulty with this step until I started thinking about antonyms. My dictionary does not suggest any antonyms for *anxious*. However, a check of some of the synonyms put me onto the trail. Here are a few of the ones I found. How does my list compare with yours?

SYNONYMS	ANTONYMS
care	assurance
insecurity	certainty
worry	confidence
concern	trust
solicitude	aplomb

Step 3—Discover Bible usages. If you were working with the King James Version, you might have been surprised to discover that the word *anxious* does not appear. What did you do then? I started checking out the synonyms and discovered several passages related to *care* and *carefulness*. That got me started. Were you able to work in a Bible dictionary or a concordance such as *Cruden's Complete Concordance* or *Young's Analytical Concordance to the Bible?* If so, did you discover several different meanings for *care* and *carefulness?* You should have discovered that some care is not worry but is interest and good will. You probably got an indication of this when working with the dictionary definition. I trust that you confined your search in the concordance to words that show a kind of care that causes worry, fret, or anxiety. We are using the *New American Standard Bible* as our basic text for this study. Did you look up the words *anxious, care,* and *worry* in the concordance of your *New American Standard Bible?* Check your findings against mine:

100

Verses that use the word anxious
- Matthew 6:25
- Matthew 6:27
- Matthew 6:31
- Matthew 6:34
- Matthew 10:19
- Mark 13:11
- Luke 12:26
- Philippians 4:6

Verses that use the word care
- Genesis 50:24
- Psalms 142:4
- Ezekiel 34:12
- Luke 10:34
- 1 Corinthians 12:25
- 1 Timothy 3:5
- 1 Peter 5:7
- Psalms 8:4
- Mark 4:38

Verses that use the word worry
- Luke 8:14
- Luke 10:41
- Luke 12:29

I hope that as you studied the various passages, you made careful notes about who was using the word and the book in which it is used. Failing to do this as a part of your study is taking a dangerous shortcut.

Another dangerous shortcut is not taking time to study the same passage in modern English translations. It helped me to see how other translations used words like *being bothered* or *fretting*. Record here one word or phrase you found that was helpful or interesting to you.

_____

Step 4—Identify the Bible meaning. As you studied these verses, you probably noticed that some of them refer to being concerned in a legitimate way. Care and concern are not always wrong. Arrange the verses you were given from the *New American Standard Bible* concordance in two lists, legitimate concern and harmful anxiety.

Legitimate Concern	Harmful Anxiety
_____	_____

_____ _____
_____ _____
_____ _____
_____ _____
_____ _____
_____ _____
_____ _____
_____ _____
_____

Step 5—Summarize. I remind you that the form in which you decided to prepare your summary is not important. However, it is important that you discovered and identified these teachings:
- How concerned should you be about things?
- What attitude should you have about the future?
- What attitude should you have about the nonessentials of life?
- What should be your attitude about life in this world?
- What does the Bible teach about trying to please the wrong people?

I hope you were careful to note that in some cases a certain amount of care is healthy and productive. In other cases, care is wrong. Did you note the cure for care that is suggested in 1 Peter 5:7?

Step 6—Plan applications. This is the step that determines whether your Bible study will be academic or life-transforming. Even though this assignment was a practice exercise, I hope you were serious enough about the study that you prayed about the applications that you would identify and that you have committed yourself to them.

In the next session, we will study the second aid, which is **UNDERSTANDING BIBLICAL IMAGES.**

WEEK 9, DAY 4

THIS UNIT: Five Aids to Understanding Bible Study
THIS TOPIC: Understanding Biblical Images

TODAY: Images of Comparison and Association

Read Micah 4:3; Matthew 5:13-14; Luke 16:29; 1 Thessalonians 2:6-7,11; James 1:6.

Sometimes the truths of the Bible are so profound that we cannot express them with normal word associations. When we encounter this, we discover that figures of speech are used in the Bible. These figures of speech present pictures and images to express the deep and difficult in a vivid, memorable manner.

Our study of the figures of speech in the Bible can help us to understand better what the Bible is saying when it uses these images. As we understand how the Bible uses images, we can improve our own communication by using similar vivid images.

Figures of speech in the Bible appear in different forms. Sometimes two items are compared to each other. On another occasion there is a deliberate understatement or an obvious overstatement. Also we can personify lifeless objects. This use of the figure of speech can add vividness to speech which might otherwise be dull. If someone asks, "Is it cold today?" the reply "Yes, it surely is cold" conveys information but does not express an arresting comparison. However, the statement "It is cold enough to freeze the sun" grips your attention.

Figures of speech normally are taken from the background of the speaker or writer who uses them. Generally, they are easily understood by both the writer and the hearer or reader. When Paul referred to himself and Timothy as bondservants of Christ Jesus, he was using a metaphor based on the practice of slavery in the New Testament world. We can increase our understanding of the figures of speech in the Bible by learning more about culture, background, and history of Bible times.

The most common images in the Bible make comparisons between two objects. A simile is a figure of speech which uses such words as *like* or *as* in comparing two unrelated objects. A metaphor also compares two unrelated objects, but it omits the use of the terms *like* or *as*.

Let's look at some metaphors in the Bible and see how they help you picture more vividly the idea the writer is trying to communicate. First, I want you to call up a mental picture. Think of a violent sea storm. Now picture one wave being driven and tossed before the wind. Concentrate on that wave. What feelings do you have? What descriptive words and phrases come to mind? Write those descriptive words and phrases on and around the wave in the drawing.

102

Now read James 1:6. How the metaphor makes the writer's words spring to life before your very eyes! Quickly, while the feelings and mental images are still fresh, write a description of a person torn by indecision.

_____

_____

Now imagine that you are looking at yourself in a mirror. Concentrate on what you see in the mirror. Visualize your face, your hair, the line of your chin. How are you dressed? Now imagine that you have walked away from the mirror and suddenly you cannot remember what you saw when you looked at yourself. No matter how hard you try, you cannot remember. What do you feel? What conclusions can you draw about yourself? What kind of a person cannot remember his own reflection in a mirror?

Read James 1:23-24. What was James saying about a person who hears God's word and then does not obey it?

_____

_____

Paul used a simile three times in 1 Thessalonians 2:6-7,11. He compared his work among the Thessalonians to the authority of an apostle, the gentleness of a nursing mother, and the earnestness of a father. Jesus used the metaphor when He addressed His followers as "the salt of the earth" and "the light of the world" (Matt. 5:13-14). James used a metaphor when he compared the tongue to a fire and when he related our earthly life to a temporary vapor which vanishes away (Jas. 3:6; 4:14). Take time to contemplate on each of these metaphors as I directed you to contemplate on the two in James 1. Catch the vividness of what the writer is trying to communicate in his metaphor.

Another figure of speech involves the use of association. In metonymy (muh-TON-uh-mē) the name of one thing is used for another thing because a cause may suggest an effect, or an effect may describe a cause. In Luke 16:29 Jesus uses the term "Moses and the Prophets" to describe the writings of which they were authors. Moses and the prophets could speak through these writings to warn the brothers of the rich fool to avoid the torment which he was experiencing.

Another figure of speech which uses association is synecdoche (suh-NEK-duh-kē). Here a part is used for a whole, or a whole is used for a part. In Acts 27:37 (KJV) the term "souls" is used for the whole man. The *New American Standard Bible* translates this word as "persons." In Micah 4:3 the abandonment of two weapons, swords and spears, stands for total disarmament.

In these images of comparison and association the truth is easy to see. The use of the figure of speech makes an otherwise dull picture vivid. It also stimulates our imagination as we consider all that is involved in the figure of speech.

Today you should begin memorizing 1 Thessalonians 4:14. Note the word imagery the writer uses.

WEEK 9, DAY 5

THIS UNIT: *Five Aids to Understanding Bible Study*
THIS TOPIC: *Understanding Biblical Images*
TODAY: *Personification and Understatement*

Read Matthew 6:34; Acts 1:25; Galatians 5:22-23; 1 Thessalonians 4:14.

We have learned that the most frequent type of image used in the Bible is comparison. Similes and metaphors are images in which two unrelated objects are compared with each other. The Bible also uses images concerned with association. In metonymy one thing is used for another, and in synecdoche a part is used for a whole. We can enrich our understanding of the images in the Bible by the study of other types of images.

The Bible uses personification. The Bible can talk about something which has no life as if it had life. Identify the personification in Matthew 6:34 and explain in your own words the idea that Jesus was trying to communicate.

_____

_____

_____

When Jesus said that "tomorrow will care for itself," He was viewing tomorrow as a living person surrounded with care and worry. The Psalms often personify the various parts of nature. The psalmist does this in Psalm 114:5-6 when he says, "What ails you, O sea, that you flee? O Jordan, that you turn back? O mountains, that you skip like rams? O hills, like lambs?" Here the sea and mountains, which have no life, appear as living beings. James uses personification in James 5:4 when he says that "the pay of the laborers who mowed your fields, and which has been withheld by you, cries out against you."

Personification expresses the deep feeling and imagination of the language in religion. Interpreting the meaning of these passages is not difficult. The writer does not actually see the quality, thing, or idea as alive, but he uses symbolic language which adds vividness and power for communication.

Another type of image which appears frequently in the Bible is understatement. Sometimes understatement is used to remove a blunt or distasteful statement from a sentence. This biblical image is called euphemism (YOU-fuh-mizem). We use euphemism in English when we say that someone has "passed away" instead of saying bluntly that "he has died." What is the euphemism in Acts 1:25?

_____

_____

104

What is the euphemism in 1 Thessalonians 4:14?

_____

When Peter urged the church to choose a replacement for Judas, he described Judas as one who had "turned aside to go to his own place." He speaks of the final destiny of Judas without any harsh, threatening suggestion. In 1 Thessalonians 4:14 Paul used euphemism when he described some deceased Thessalonian Christians as "those who have fallen asleep in Jesus." These Christians were not literally asleep. In death they look as if they are asleep, but in truth they are with Jesus. We will use this as a memory verse to remind us of our great hope for life after death.

Another type of understatement is meiosis (my-Ō-sis). This is the use of understatement to call attention to a comment or an idea. In meiosis a negative statement often is used to declare a positive truth. Find the meiosis in the following passages. What is the writer actually saying?

Galatians 5:22-23 _____

_____

_____

1 Thessalonians 2:15 _____

_____

_____

In this passage Paul listed the fruits of the Spirit, a collection of godly character traits which the Holy Spirit can produce in the life of a Christian. He concludes his list of these fruits by saying that "against such things there is no law." This is a deliberate understatement. No law enforcement agency would need to protect its citizens against love, joy, peace, and self-control. Paul's understatement calls attention to the godly influence of the fruits of the Spirit.

In 1 Thessalonians 2:15 Paul described the Jews as people who killed the Lord Jesus and the prophets and drove away Christian preachers who attempted to declare the truth. Then he adds, "They are not pleasing to God." This again is a deliberate understatement. By such an understatement he calls attention to just how much the Jews angered or displeased God.

To determine the presence of understatement, a student must concentrate and reflect on what the Bible is actually saying. Wherever a statement or comment is so obviously true that it doesn't need to be stated, the writers of the Bible have practiced understatement for effect and emphasis.

WEEK 10, DAY 1

THIS UNIT: *Five Aids to Understanding Bible Study*
THIS TOPIC: *Understanding Biblical Images*
TODAY: *Overstatement and Interrogation*

Read Matthew 5:30; 27:29; Romans 6:1; 2 Corinthians 8:2; Colossians 1:6.

We have learned that the Bible can use understatement and personification effectively to communicate its truth. Today we will learn two additional types of images which can call attention to the beliefs of the biblical writers.

One type of overstatement is known as hyperbole (hī-PUR-buh-lē). This is an intentional overstatement for emphasis and communication. Hyperbole occurs in all languages and is very effective. Paul used hyperbole when he said that the gospel had gone into "all the world" (Col. 1:6). The Christian message had not gone into every geographic corner of the world. However, it had spread over the inhabited world. No one would accuse Paul of error. He was describing vividly the wide and rapid spread of Christianity.

Also, we have seen that Jesus used hyperbole when He said, "If your right hand makes you stumble, cut it off, and throw it from you" (Matt. 5:30). No one should literally remove his right hand. However, he must show the same zeal in fighting sin which he might show if he did remove the hand (see week 3, day 5).

John used hyperbole when he said that if all the events of Jesus' life were written down "even the world itself would not contain the books which were written" (John 21:25). John had stated that the deeds of Jesus were much more numerous than he had written. He impressed his audience that he had been selective in writing his account of Jesus' life.

Another figure of speech which involves overstatement is called the oxymoron (ox-i-MŌR-on). Here is a figure of speech in which opposite or contradictory ideas appear. We use this figure of speech in English when we speak of a thunderous silence. The union of these opposing ideas can have an arresting effect on readers. Paul used this image when he described the Macedonian Christians as people whose "deep poverty overflowed in the wealth of their liberality" (2 Cor. 8:2). Poverty doesn't normally lead to generosity. When Paul combined the two ideas, he expressed a gripping thought which claims our attention.

The Bible also uses irony. This is a figure of speech when the words show the opposite of the true intent of the writer. If you jump into icy water, you may have someone ask you, "How's the water?" You may answer "Fine!" through clenched, chattering teeth, and you mean the very opposite of what you are saying. This is irony. The Roman soldiers used irony when they welcomed Jesus with the words, "'Hail, King of the Jews'" (Matt. 27:29). The Jews actually felt scorn and contempt, but their words showed a pretended form of worship.

Sometimes the Bible uses a figure of speech when it asks a question. The writer asks these questions for effect and purpose. Occasionally the answer is obvious, and the question has become the means of directing the thought toward a central idea. Paul used this method in Romans 6:1 when he said: "What shall we say then? Are we to continue in sin that grace might increase?" Paul quickly answered his question with the words, "May it never be!" The answer to the question was clear already. He used the question to draw our attention to an idea. This kind of question is known as a rhetorical question.

These figures of speech make the reading of the Bible more vivid and interesting. However, the biblical writers did not merely use the figures of speech as decorations. They were a part of the effort to teach the truth and oppose error. Our learning these figures of speech can help to make us more effective in our own presentation of God's message.

This concludes your study of a number of figures of speech that Bible writers used to communicate their ideas more vividly. I'm sure you see how understanding figures of speech will greatly enhance your understanding of the Bible.

Let's review before we begin studying the next area. Match each of the following figures of speech with the correct definition from the list on the right.

_____ 1. synecdoche

_____ 2. rhetorical question

_____ 3. irony

_____ 4. metaphor

_____ 5. euphemism

_____ 6. meiosis

_____ 7. simile

_____ 8. oxymoron

_____ 9. personification

_____ 10. hyperbole

_____ 11. metonymy

a. Comparing one object to another using *like* or *as*.

b. Comparing one object to another without using *like* or *as*.

c. Using the name of one person or object to represent another person or object.

d. Using a part to represent the whole or vice versa.

e. Speaking of an inanimate object as if it had life.

f. Using understatement to soften the blunt or distasteful nature of a statement.

g. Using a negative statement to declare a positive truth.

h. Using exaggeration or overstatement.

i. Exaggerating or overstating the opposite idea from the truth you are stating.

j. Using a statement that expresses the opposite of what you actually feel.

k. Asking a question for which the answer is obvious.

1-*d*; 2-*k*; 3-*j*; 4-*b*; 5-*f*; 6-*g*; 7-*a*; 8-*i*; 9-*e*; 10-*h*; 11-*c*

Your first Scripture memory assignment for this week is Matthew 7:7.

WEEK 10, DAY 2

THIS UNIT: *Five Aids to Understanding Bible Study*
THIS TOPIC: *Understanding the Grammar of the Bible*
TODAY: *The Grammatical Form of a Statement*

Read Matthew 7:7; 28:19-20; Philippians 1:21; Hebrews 3:12.

As you try to understand the Bible, one area which can provide much assistance is a knowledge of grammar. I will not give you a complete English lesson, but I will use some simple examples from grammar to give added depth to your Bible study. Grammatical study is not something which you will do by itself. You will use it to add to other types of study such as synthetic and analytical study (see weeks 4 and 5).

In this session I want to review with you the four kinds of statements you deal with in the Bible and review your Scripture memorization at the same time. If you do not remember the four kinds of statements, review the material found in week 3 of this study. In this session's material, you will find four note cards. Each note card identifies one type of statement, explains it, and calls for a Scripture reference to serve as an example. From memory, you are to supply one or more Scripture references that illustrate that kind of statement.

TYPE: Statement of fact
NOTES:

This form of statement appears in books that deal with historical matters such as 1 and 2 Samuel and Acts. It also appears in the epistles of Paul, Peter, and John. In Philippians 1:21 Paul states, "To me, to live is Christ, and to die is gain." Paul is stating his view of life's most important priority.

Some early Christians tried to see a symbol of Jesus' victory on the cross in the number 318 of Genesis 14:14. The Bible is not using that number to point to Jesus. It is merely saying that Abraham took 318 men to fight.

EXAMPLE REFERENCE(S): _____

_____

TYPE: Warning
NOTES:

A warning is an alarm or a signal to avoid something. In the Bible a warning appears frequently with the words *beware* or *take heed* used to introduce the warning. When we see warnings, we know that these statements contain advice which we must apply. The Book of Hebrews contains many warnings and expresses one with the words: "Take heed, . . . lest there be in any of you an evil heart of unbelief, in departing from the living God" (Heb. 3:12, KJV). Jesus used warnings when He alerted His disciples to the dangers of false teachers in Matthew 7:15.

EXAMPLE REFERENCE(S) WITH AN IMPLIED WARNING: _____

_____

TYPE: Promise
NOTES:

We can apply the promises of the Bible to our own lives unless a specific promise applies to someone else or is limited to another time. If the promise comes with conditions, we must follow those conditions in order to reap the promise (see also week 3, day 3). When Jesus says in Matthew 7:7 to "'ask, and it shall be given to you,'" we must endure and persist in the practice of prayer before we can have assurance that God will hear our prayer. Memorize this verse as an incentive to add persistence to your prayer life. God's promise in Acts 27:22-24 that no man on the ship with Paul would die applied personally to Paul. If we are in danger, we might hope for the same kind of protection, but we cannot command God to do it.

EXAMPLE REFERENCE(S): _____

TYPE: Command
NOTES:

Both a command and a warning are spoken with a sense of obligation and order to the reader. The difference between these two is that the warning sounds an alarm, and the command is a specific call to action. One of Jesus' most notable commands is the Great Commission in Matthew 28:19: "Go ye therefore, and teach all nations, baptizing them in the name of the Father, and of the Son, and of the Holy Ghost" (KJV). Jesus is calling all of His followers to action and is not merely sending out a signal of danger. Peter gave a command when he said, "Like the Holy One who called you, be holy yourselves also in all your behavior" (1 Pet. 1:15).

EXAMPLE REFERENCE(S): _____

The second Scripture memory assignment for this week is Titus 2:11-13. Begin memorizing it today because it is longer than usual.

WEEK 10, DAY 3

THIS UNIT: *Five Aids to Understanding Bible Study*
THIS TOPIC: *Understanding the Grammar of the Bible*
TODAY: *Understanding Connectives*

Read Matthew 26:32; 2 Thessalonians 2:15; 1 John 2:12; 5:13.

Suppose that I say to you, "I didn't come to your party because I was sick." The last three words of the sentence explain why I didn't come to the party. The word *because* is a connective introducing those three words, *I was sick*. Connectives are words which join together the parts of sentences. We call each part of the above sentence a clause because each part has a subject and a verb in it. The connectives join the clauses of the sentence together. There are many types of connectives, and each type can give us some different information about what the biblical writer is trying to tell us.

Some connectives show TIME. There are at least four in this group. Read the following passages and identify the connective in each. Note the chronological relationship of events that the connective establishes.

Matthew 26:32 _____

Acts 19:1 _____

1 Timothy 1:12-13 _____

Acts 2:37 _____

When a biblical writer uses one of the connectives *after, before, when,* or *while,* he is placing the events of one of the clauses either before, after, or at the same time as the events of another clause. Sometimes it is important in reading and understanding the Bible just to know the time relations between various clauses. Observing the time connectives can help you to understand this.

Some connectives show the REASON BEHIND CERTAIN ACTIONS. There are at least three connectives in this group. Read the following passages and identify the connective. Note the relationship between cause and effect.

1 John 2:12 _____

2 Corinthians 13:2-3 _____

2 Corinthians 4:18—5:4 _____

The connectives *because, since,* and *for* show the relationship between cause and effect, with the emphasis on the cause. When you see these connectives in a statement, you know that the writer is probably saying, "*Because of the reason I am stating*, this result is taking place." The next group of connectives reverses the emphasis.

Some connectives INTRODUCE OR SHOW RESULTS. At least three connectives are in this group. Examine the following passages and identify the connective in each. Again, note carefully the relationship between cause and effect.

2 Thessalonians 2:14-15 _____

Galatians 6:2 _____

1 Corinthians 14:24-25 _____

The connectives *then, so,* and *thus* also show relationship between cause and effect, but with the emphasis on the effect. When a biblical writer uses one of these connectives, he is probably saying,

"Because of the reason I am stating, *this result is taking place.*"

The final group of connectives shows PURPOSE. The two previous groups of connectives stressed either cause or effect in the relationship between two actions or occurrences. The next connectives are distinctive from the others because they emphasize the PURPOSE or REASON for an action being taken. At least two connectives are in this group. Read the following passages and identify the connective in each.

1 John 5:13 _____

Hebrews 13:6 _____

As you read and study the Scriptures, you should note the time relationships, the relationship between cause and effect, and the reasons or purposes that are indicated by the way connectives are used. Often, the clue you receive from the connective that is used will make the difference in the way you understand and interpret a passage.

WHEN JESUS SAID, "I AM COME <u>THAT</u> THEY MIGHT HAVE LIFE" (KJV), HE WAS STRESSING _____

WHEN PAUL SAID, "<u>WHILE</u> WE WERE YET SINNERS, CHRIST DIED FOR US" (KJV), HE WAS STRESSING _____

WHEN JOHN SAID, "WE LOVE HIM, <u>BECAUSE</u> HE FIRST LOVED US" (KJV), HE WAS STRESSING _____

WHEN PAUL SAID, "<u>SO THEN</u>, BRETHREN, STAND FIRM AND HOLD TO THE TRADITIONS WHICH YOU WERE TAUGHT," HE WAS STRESSING _____

WEEK 10, DAY 4

THIS UNIT: *Five Aids to Understanding Bible Study*
THIS TOPIC: *Understanding the Grammar of the Bible*
TODAY: *Understanding the Parts of Speech*

Read Matthew 16:18; Acts 8:4; 1 Corinthians 3:6; 11:18.

Understanding the basic rules of grammar and the relationships among the different parts of speech will enhance the effectiveness and skill with which you can use the other kinds of Bible study that you have been practicing during the weeks of this study.

English has eight parts of speech, but we will notice only five of them in our study. We will use the verb, noun, pronoun, adjective, and adverb.

A verb shows action or existence. Verbs also have tense. In English this means that they show time relationships. Verbs can speak of something which is happening now, has already happened in the past, or will happen in the future. We call these tenses present, past, and future. Observing the tense of a statement is important in understanding and applying what it means. In 1 Corinthians 11:18 Paul wrote, "I hear that divisions exist among you." We can feel those differences seething at that time within the church at Corinth. In Ephesians 2:1 Paul said, "You were dead in your trespasses and sins." That fact had been true of Paul's readers in the past, but now they were alive unto Christ. In John 14:26 Jesus promised that the Holy Spirit "will teach you all things." That promise holds true in our own future relationship with God through Christ. As we live with Him in days ahead, the Holy Spirit will teach us things about God which we need to know.

Now here is an interesting question for you. At what point does salvation take place? Check the answer that you think is correct.
[ ] You were saved at the moment you repented of your sin and trusted Christ for salvation.
[ ] Your salvation is now in progress and is a daily process.
[ ] Your salvation will take place at some time in the future.

You answered correctly only if you checked all three! Study 2 Corinthians 1:9-10. Use the King James Version for the study, noting carefully the verb tenses in verse 10. Then fill in the following chart.

THREE TENSES OF SALVATION	
"We had the sentence of death in ourselves, that we should not trust in ourselves, but in God which raiseth the dead:	
PAST	who _____ us from so great a death,
PRESENT	and _____ .
FUTURE	in whom we trust that he _____ us."

Scripture teaches that there are three aspects to your salvation—one that has already taken place, another that is now taking place, and a third that will take place in the future. Verb tenses in Scripture help us understand these and other Bible truths.

Verbs have an active and a passive voice. The active voice shows the subject acting or carrying out the action. The passive voice shows the subject receiving the action. In 1 Corinthians 3:6 Paul said, "I planted, Apollos watered, but God was causing the growth." God was the active cause of the spread of the gospel in Corinth. In Ephesians 2:8 Paul added, "By grace you have been saved through faith." We do not save ourselves, but we receive God's mercy.

A noun is the name of a person, place, or a thing. A proper noun is the name of a particular person, place, or thing. The names of people are proper nouns, and in the Bible these names often describe the spiritual potential of the individual. The name *Jesus* means *savior,* and the name *Peter* means *rock* (Matt. 16:18). Some proper nouns used as place names also describe something about the significance of the location. The term *Decapolis* in Mark 7:31 means *ten cities*. It is a reference to ten Greek cities across the Jordan River where pagan influence was felt in New Testament days. In Acts 1:19 the name *Hakeldama* means *field of blood* and refers to the field in which Judas Iscariot took his life. You often can find the meaning of a proper name by using a concordance.

Pronouns are words used in place of nouns. The word for which the pronoun stands is called its antecedent. In Acts 8:4 Luke describes a group of people by saying, "Those who had been scattered went about preaching the word." The antecedent of *those* appears in verse 1. It refers not to the apostles but to ordinary Christians driven from Jerusalem by the persecutions of Jews. Ordinary Christians were spreading the gospel.

Adjectives modify nouns and pronouns. Adverbs modify verbs, adjectives, and other adverbs. Their presence in a sentence adds life and vitality to expressions which could otherwise be dull. In 1 Peter 1:4 Peter uses adjectives to describe our Christian inheritance as "imperishable and undefiled and will not fade away." These vivid words describe a reward which cannot be taken away with the passage of time, appearance of decay, or presence of failure. In Titus 2:12 Paul uses adverbs to urge us to live "sensibly, righteously and godly." These words picture someone who has self-restraint and complete commitment to God.

This concludes your study of the third aid to understanding Bible study. You have now studied the importance of understanding (1) words, (2) biblical images, and (3) the grammar of the Bible. Tomorrow we will begin studying how to **UNDERSTAND TOPICS IN THE BIBLE.**

WEEK 10, DAY 5

THIS UNIT: **Five Aids to Understanding Bible Study**
THIS TOPIC: **Understanding Topics in the Bible**
TODAY: **Why Study and Understand Topics**

Your Reading Assignment Will Come Later.

We have not done a general review recently. Perhaps we should get our bearings by doing one now. We will not do a detailed review until the end of the study. Let's review only the main areas or units that you have studied. By this time you should be able to label each finger on the hand diagram we have been using as the organizer for the study. Take time now to review by listing the areas you have studied. If you have difficulty recalling any units, look back in your book.

The area we are studying now is **FIVE AIDS TO UNDERSTANDING BIBLE STUDY.** So far, we have studied three. Can you list them?

_____

_____

_____

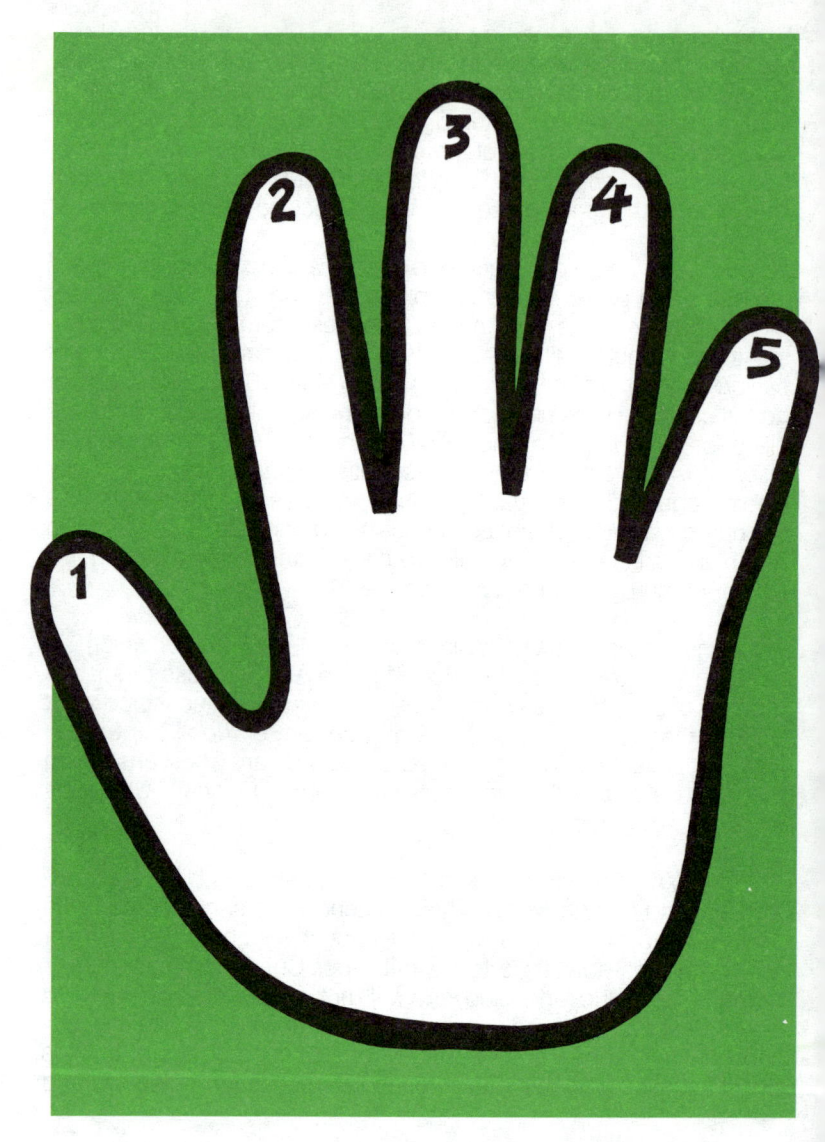

Today we begin studying the fourth aid: **UNDERSTANDING TOPICS IN THE BIBLE.** Topical Bible study is the study of the topical teachings in the Bible. You may limit the topic to a single book, such as a study of the teaching in the Book of James about the use of the tongue. You also may trace the topic throughout Scripture, such as a study of the miracles in the Bible. The topic can be narrow, such as prophecies about Jesus' birth, or it can be broad and lengthy, such as prophecies in the Bible. A topical study can include topics which are important for churches, such as the role and requirements for church leaders. Husbands and wives can study the biblical topics of parenting and husband-wife relationships. Business persons can learn the topic of what the Bible says about handling money. Teachers can study Jesus' principles of teaching.

Topical Bible study can involve the study of a doctrine, such as the nature of God or the work of the Holy Spirit. It also can involve a practical matter, such as the ministries of a local church. Topical study is not just a type of study which will satisfy curiosity. In any instance of topical study the focus must be on what the topic can provide for personal application.

Topical Bible study is important because it provides for a logical and orderly method of studying the Bible. The instructions and guidelines of the Bible appear throughout the Scriptures. A student can use the topical method of study to bring together in an orderly manner all that the Bible teaches about the use of time, money, or any other suitable topic. Also, the use of topical Bible study can provide a balanced understanding of biblical teaching. For example, Galatians 6:2 says, "Bear one another's burdens, and thus fulfill the law of Christ." In contrast, Galatians 6:5 warns, "Each one shall bear his own load." A study of a topic such as encouraging other Christians can help you to know which burdens you should bear and which burdens require help.

Topical Bible study also provides variety in individual study of the Scriptures. There is no limit to the varieties of topics available for individual study. It is a type of study which fits well with the study of a book in the Bible. After you have studied a book such as 1 Peter, you can study it again to look at such topics as God's directions for meeting suffering, the Christian and government, the duties of church leaders, and the example of Christ. This study will enrich what you already have learned from your own investigation of the message in the entire book. Topical Bible study helps the student apply the Bible to daily living.

Some reference Bibles already have done much of the work which would be necessary for topical study of the Bible. *The Thompson Chain-Reference Bible Survey* contains many varieties of topical studies listed in the back of the Bible. These references contain verses of Scripture in which you can continue to investigate the topic which appears. You will need only to look up the references.

The Holman *Master Study Bible* contains an encyclopedia that will prove helpful in topical Bible study.

The method of topical study which we will follow will teach you to use a concordance or a topical Bible to do your own study. The encouragement and excitement which you will receive as you do your personal investigation can become an incentive to spur your own interest in Bible study.

Now here is your reading assignment for this session. I have an additional assignment to go with it. I want you to read the Book of James. As you do, identify topics you might want to study. On the following chart, list each topic and record the chapter and verses that deal with that topic.

POSSIBLE TOPICS FOR STUDY	
Topic	Reference

WEEK 11, DAY 1

THIS UNIT: *Five Aids to Understanding Bible Study*
THIS TOPIC: *Understanding Topics in the Bible*
TODAY: *How to Study and Understand Topics*

Your Reading Assignment Will Come Later.

After you complete your two Scripture memory assignments for this week, you will have memorized thirty-two verses in twenty-two different passages. Good for you! You have done well. Your first assignment for this week is Matthew 18:15.

Topical Bible study enables us to assemble the teachings of the Bible on a subject which interests us. This type of study can provide an overview of the teachings in the Bible instead of letting the material remain isolated and independent.

The topic which you select should be one in which you have a spiritual interest or one about which you have a need to gather information. After you select the topic, your first step is to make a list of words such as synonyms, phrases, or ideas which have something in common with your topic. If you are studying the topic of "the tongue," you might list such related terms as *words, speaking, boasting, cursing, blessing, utterance, instruction, reproof,* or *words of knowledge.* All of these terms are related to the general idea of the tongue.

After you have made a list of words, you can use a concordance and a topical Bible to find Bible references to your topic. For example, *Young's Analytical Concordance to the Bible* has nearly one hundred Old Testament references to the word *tongue* and over fifty New Testament references to the topic. As you collect these verses, you will want to use only those verses which relate to your topic. Some of the references in the New Testament to the tongue are referring to a spoken language and do not offer moral instruction about the tongue. Words such as *blessing* and *boasting* will show different ways of using the tongue. In looking at these words, however, be selective in choosing among the verses which describe the types of tongue usage. If your interest concerns the spiritual use of the tongue, add only those verses which help you to understand this topic.

After you have collected the references, write down an observation, a comment, or a question about each reference. Notice that the model I suggested for a worksheet has a special section for listing references and comments. Be certain that your comments accurately reflect the context of the verses. Your comments can concern the meaning of important words in the verse, any insight about why the verse was written, and how it applies to your life. Do not fail to include questions about issues which you don't understand.

After you have gathered all the references, you will notice that some of them relate to the same section of your topic. In studying the topic of the tongue you will find, for example, that some verses speak about good uses of the tongue, bad uses of the tongue, controlling the tongue, or God's judgment of the tongue. You will want to use another sheet of paper to group together those verses which treat the same subdivision of the topic.

After you have grouped the references together, you can arrange the material into an outline. As you review the material which you have gathered, a logical division of it will become clear to you. It is probably best to make your outline with several subdivisions under main topics. Each subdivision should contain a listing of the references to those verses which support that subdivision. This type of activity will provide you with an outline which you can use in teaching or sharing your ideas with others.

You can conclude your study by summarizing the outline which you make. The outline will provide you with a complete view of what you have studied. The summary will help you to condense what you have learned into a few words. Your conclusion should contain not only a summary of teaching but also ideas for personal or group application.

In studying some subjects, you may want to provide a limit to your research by restricting your study to one book. A study of the tongue can be a broad study. Both the Books of Proverbs and James have extensive teaching on the use of the tongue. Helpful insight about the use and abuse of the tongue can be found from a study of either one of the books.

I want to suggest a plan sheet to use for doing a topical Bible study. You will note that it is very similar to some of the other worksheets I have suggested. Prepare the front just as I have illustrated it here. Prepare the back as you prepared the backs of the other worksheets.

TOPICAL BIBLE STUDY WORKSHEET
TOPIC: _____

Related words:	
Outline	Summary

WEEK 11, DAY 2

THIS UNIT: *Five Aids to Understanding Bible Study*
THIS TOPIC: *Understanding Topics in the Bible*
TODAY: *A Practice Topical Bible Study*

Read Passages Related to Confrontation in the Experiences of Jesus, Paul, and Peter.

At this session I want us to follow a procedure that we have followed before by having you work on your own and then compare notes with me. Take time now to do a topical study of confrontation in the experiences of Jesus, Paul, and Peter. You should gather all the Bible study resources available to you, and you should prepare a worksheet like the one I suggested to you at the previous session. Put this book aside and do your study. Then come back, and we will compare notes.

WORK ON YOUR OWN TO COMPLETE
THE BIBLE STUDY BEFORE
READING FURTHER IN THIS BOOK

Several years ago I listened with interest to a speaker who said that confrontation was an important ministry for any Christian. He defined confrontation as a word of encouragement or warning given by one Christian to another in need. His message sparked my interest in learning what the Bible taught about confrontation.

I began my study by listing phrases, ideas, or synonyms which related to the idea of confrontation. Among some of these words were *exhort (exhortation), encourage, support,* and *rebuke.* Can you list other words or phrases besides these?

I looked through the Bible to find references on the subject of confrontation by using a concordance. Among the verses which I selected were Acts 20:2; 1 Timothy 5:1,20; and 1 Thessalonians 5:14. In addition to using a concordance, I read selectively through portions of the Bible in which spiritual leaders were confronting their followers and urging them to action. I quickly realized that so much material was available to study confrontation that it would be better to limit it to the New Testament. Knowing that so much material in the Bible is related to confrontation is the reason that I began by limiting your assignment to confrontation in the experiences of Jesus, Paul, and Peter. For this limited area alone, I found passages dealing with confrontation from the life of Jesus, the ministry of Paul, and the leadership of Peter. Among examples are Matthew 4:19; Matthew 13:54-58; Matthew 18:15-17; Mark 2:1-12; Mark 8:33; Mark 11:15-18; Mark 14:35-36; Luke 16:14-15; Acts 1:15-26; 2:14-40; 5:1-11; 7:51-52; 9:4-6; 9:15-16; Romans 16:17; 1 Corinthians 5:3-5,13; Galatians 1:10; Titus 3:10-11; Hebrews 10:24-25; and James 2:1. Some of these passages find persons confronting persons. Others show God and persons talking about needs and problems. How does this group of references compare with the ones you listed on your worksheet? Circle all the ones I listed that you did not list on your worksheet. You may want to add these to your list. Did you include references on your worksheet that I did not list? If so, list those here.

_____

_____

_____

As I used these questions in my own study, I was able to get a better understanding of a number of facts. For example, in Matthew 18:15-17 Jesus gave instructions for confronting a brother who has

QUESTIONS:
WHO IS DOING THE CONFRONTING?
WHO IS BEING CONFRONTED?
WHY IS THE CONFRONTATION NECESSARY?
WHAT METHOD OF CONFRONTATION IS USED?
WHAT ARE THE RESULTS OF THE CONFRONTATION?

sinned or strayed. The method used is direct personal encounter. Matthew 18:15 is our first memory verse for the week. In Hebrews 10:24-25 the writer of Hebrews confronts an entire church. The confronting was necessary because members of the church were becoming careless and falling into disobedience. Use these examples to evaluate the kinds of observations you made as you studied.

The next step was to formulate an outline. Let me show you how I began my outline to give you an idea of how yours should look. I am providing the first part of the outline. Complete the outline.

I. Jesus and the ministry of confrontation
   1. Jesus confronted hypocrisy (Luke 16:14-15)
   2. Jesus challenged others to action (Matt. 4:19)
   3. Jesus challenged others to gain greater understanding (Mark 8:33)

II. Paul _____

III. Peter _____

The last two steps in your study are more personal than the preceding steps because they reflect needs you feel. It is quite possible that your summary statements were something like these.
- The church must practice the ministry of confrontation to prevent believers from slipping into sin (Matt. 18:15-17; 1 Cor. 5:3-5,13).
- The aim of confrontation is to challenge a believer to practice love and good works (Heb. 10:24-25).

You can add other summaries in addition to those listed. These summaries will give you material which you can use in personal or group application.

This concludes your study of understanding the topics of the Bible. At the next session you will begin studying the final subject in the last major division of the study.

119

WEEK 11, DAY 3

THIS UNIT: *Five Aids to Understanding Bible Study*
THIS TOPIC: *Understanding Doctrines in the Bible*
TODAY: *Types of Doctrinal Bible Study*

Read 1 Corinthians 15:1-23; 2 Corinthians 5:1; 1 Thessalonians 5:2; Philippians.

Take a quick quiz. Use *T* or *F* to indicate whether you think each of the following statements is true or false.
____ Truths of the Bible are easy to understand because they are presented in such a systematic, organized manner.
____ Some biblical truths can be discovered by carefully reading the Bible.
____ Careful examination of Scripture reveals that the writers of the Bible carefully avoided making assumptions.
____ Surprisingly, no blocks of Scripture are purely theological in content.
As you study this session, you will surely discover how you should have responded to the quiz. But I will give you the correct responses at the end of the session just the same.

Doctrinal Bible study is an effort to learn what the Bible teaches or assumes about such topics as God, Christ, the Holy Spirit, man, salvation, and the church. Doctrinal Bible study tries to fit together what the Bible teaches about these various topics.

The Bible itself is not systematic. Its teachings about God and Christ don't appear in a logical order. We will practice doctrinal Bible study in order to fit together what the Bible says in its statements about God's truth. Until we do this, the teachings of the Bible will appear disconnected. Our study of the doctrines in the Bible can help to fit them into an order which we can teach to others.

At least three types of doctrinal study are in the Bible. The Bible writers assumed many teachings and beliefs about God without a formal statement. The writers of the Bible assumed the existence of God. They did not argue for it, seek to prove it, or labor about the issue. They assumed it.

We can discover other assumptions when we read the books of the Bible very carefully. For example, in 1 Thessalonians 1:4 Paul said that he knew God's choice of the Thessalonians. Paul was assuming that his readers were God's elect, God's children. In 1 Thessalonians 5:2 he mentioned that it is common knowledge that "the day of the Lord will come just like a thief in the night." He assumed that Jesus' return would be unexpected and without announcement.

We can uncover the beliefs and assumptions of a Bible writer by reading a book of the Bible several times. As we read, we must think carefully about what the writer is saying.

In 1 Corinthians 15:1-23 Paul assumed that Jesus' resurrection is evidence that the Christian has life after death. He stated this plainly in verses 20-23. It is a logical conclusion from his words. We can discover information such as this by careful reading of the words in Scripture.

Sometimes a Bible writer spoke to his readers with the words *we know*. . . . Paul did this in 2 Corinthians 5:1, and his use of "we know" shows a belief or an assumption which he makes. We can learn some of the assumptions of a writer by looking for statements such as this. In his Letter to the Philippians, Paul made a number of assumptions which you can discover by a careful reading of the book. Discover and list at least four of those assumptions.

1. _____

2. _____

3. _____

4. _____

A second type of doctrinal study is to collect information on subjects or topics which are prominent in a given book or text. The Book of Ephesians deals in detail with the doctrine of the church. The Book of Hebrews teaches the humanity of Christ. This type of doctrinal study closely resembles topical study. It follows many principles of topical study. It differs from topical study only in that it is a study of a doctrine or a theological statement. Doctrinal study makes an effort to understand what the Bible is teaching about God, His ways, and His plans. We use doctrinal study to increase our understanding about God's work and His will.

A third type of doctrinal study gives detailed treatment to those sections of a book which are largely doctrinal in their content. James 2:14-26 speaks about the relationship between faith and works. Romans 3:21-31 teaches justification by faith. We can turn to Hebrews 11 to understand the true nature of faith in God. The topic of the resurrection of Christ has a full treatment in 1 Corinthians 15. We can learn the content of these passages by using analytical study of the Bible to study closely doctrinal sections.

In our next two days we will learn more about the second and third types of doctrinal Bible study. We can practice the first type of doctrinal study by a careful reading of the Bible itself.

You should begin your final Scripture memory assignment today. Begin memorizing Hebrews 2:18.

Now here are the correct responses to the quiz: 1-F, 2-T, 3-F, 4-F.

WEEK 11, DAY 4

THIS UNIT: *Five Aids to Understanding Bible Study*
THIS TOPIC: *Understanding Doctrines in the Bible*
TODAY: *Discovering What One Book Says About a Doctrine*

Read Hebrews 2:17-18; 4:14-16; 5:1-10; 7:23-26.

Yesterday you learned how to do a doctrinal study simply by discovering the assumptions of the writer. Today you will learn how to study what one book says about a certain doctrine.

To learn the doctrinal teaching of a single book of Scripture, your first step is to read the book carefully several times. Each reading will help you understand a teaching or an emphasis which the book makes about God, Christ, salvation, the church, or the Holy Spirit. If you want to trace a subject of doctrine through a certain book, you should be certain that you use a book which treats the subject thoroughly. You would not want to use the Book of James to study the Holy Spirit. That is not a major emphasis in James. However, James does make several references to the second coming of Christ and to events which happen when Jesus returns (1:12; 4:12; 5:7; 5:9). You can learn where to find full discussions of doctrinal topics by reading about those topics in a Bible dictionary or encyclopedia. There you will learn which books treat the subjects in some detail.

As you study a subject in a book of the Bible, select those passages which treat the subject in which you have an interest. Sometimes you can look up in a concordance the word in which you are interested as it is found in that book of the Bible. Sometimes you cannot find the word; in that case, you will have to read carefully through a book to learn what it teaches about the doctrine.

At this session I want you to discover what the Book of Hebrews says about the humanity of Christ. As I told you at the previous session, doing this kind of study can require a great deal of time. So I am going to help you take a few shortcuts.

Prepare a worksheet like the one you prepared for topical Bible study in day 1 of this week.

You should read the book several times and identify the passages that deal with Christ's humanity. I will help you by telling you that the relevant passages are the ones that you read at the beginning of the session. Read quickly through the book so that you will understand the context of each passage. List the relevant passages on your worksheet. Then study each passage and record your comments. You may need to practice some of the principles of analytical Bible study (week 5) if you find that you have difficulty dealing with any of the passages. Also, you may need to look for more information in a commentary or some other Bible study resource. However, you should not do this until you have worked through your own personal insights.

BEFORE YOU READ FURTHER, STUDY THE PASSAGES AND RECORD YOUR COMMENTS.

The insights you gained should equip you to complete the following statements about the humanity of Christ. Some of them may seem to be similar, but each clarifies a different aspect of the humanity of Christ.

- 4:15: Christ can sympathize with the weakness of human beings because _____

_____

- 2:17: Christ's participation in the human condition allows Him to _____

_____

- 2:18; 4:15-16: Because of Christ's demonstration of obedience, He is able to _____

_____

_____

- 2:18; 4:15-16: Because Christ did not sin in the midst of His temptation, He is able to offer believers _____

_____

- 5:8: Christ learned the full meaning of obedience by _____

_____

_____

- 7:25: Because Christ lives to intercede for us, _____

_____

_____

_____

_____

Now compare your outline to the one that follows. Perhaps you can improve this outline by adding to it ideas from the outline that you have done. And perhaps you can use some ideas from this outline to improve yours.

The Helpfulness of Christ's Humanity

1. His sufferings taught Him the full meaning of obedience. (5:8-10)
   - They secured for Him a maturity in His obedience.
   - They gave Him every qualification for His priesthood.
   - They obtained a glory from the Father in His exaltation.
2. His own experiences provide encouragement for believers. (2:17-18; 4:15-16)
   - They show an example for victory.
   - They allow mercy and grace for the tempted.
3. His atonement prevents separation from God for believers. (2:17)
4. His intercession secures complete salvation for believers. (7:25)

Let me emphasize again that it is not necessary that your outline and summary be like mine. The important thing is that they focus on the central ideas that you have learned from your study and that they give guidance for applying your study.

Today you should continue to work on memorizing Hebrews 2:18.

WEEK 11, DAY 5

THIS UNIT: *Five Aids to Understanding Bible Study*
THIS TOPIC: *Understanding Doctrines in the Bible*
TODAY: *How to Study a Doctrinal Passage*

Read James 2:14-26.

Today we will give attention to studying those passages of a book in the Bible which treat a special doctrine or teach an important emphasis. This type of doctrinal Bible study is really a special type of analytical Bible study which deals with a passage which is chiefly doctrinal.

Let's use this type of study to understand the doctrine which James is teaching in James 2:14-26. Our first step in the study is to perform a careful analytical study of the passage. To refresh your mind on analytical study, refer to the material from week 5. After you have made observations, you will want to write out your own paraphrase or interpretation of the verses. You also will want to write an application of the passage in your own life.

You will want to include these observations:
- Notice that the *New American Standard Bible* translates James 2:14 as "Can that faith save him?" How does this differ from merely saying, "Can faith save him?"
- What is the meaning of the word "justified" in James 2:21,24?
- To what kind of problem is James addressing the words?
- Study the Old Testament passages (Gen. 15:6; 22:1-19) in which Abraham is mentioned. Notice that the incident of Genesis 15:6 mentioned in James 2:23 occurred before the incident of Genesis 22:1-19 mentioned in James 2:21. According to James, what did the incident in Genesis 22:1-19 prove about the incident in Genesis 15:6?
- In what sense was Rahab justified by her deeds? Look up information about her in Joshua 2.

The interpretation or paraphrase of the verses is an activity which you can undertake after your own careful reading and meditation on the verses. The application of the verses will demand careful thought from you. Notice that James 2:14-20 shows the nature of a dead faith. This kind of faith can't meet human needs and can't show an inquirer that it is genuine. In James 2:21-26 we see that genuine faith causes an obedient life. This kind of faith led Abraham to show his obedience to God by offering Isaac and also led Rahab to offer protection to the Jewish spies. What kind of modern application would you make to your own life based on these words?

In correlating this passage, you must consider the relationship of this teaching to such passages as Romans 3:21-31; Ephesians 2:8-10; and Galatians 2:17-21. Notice the close similarity in wording between the Romans passage and the passage here. Paul says that we are "justified by faith," while James says that we are "justified by works." Is there a difference in the meaning of the word *justify* as used by Paul and James? How would you define each man's use of the word?

To conclude this type of doctrinal Bible study, you can summarize in a sentence or two what the passage in James 2:14-26 teaches.

This brings us to the end of fifty-five sessions together. I am grateful to you for the way you have applied yourself. Before we close the book, how about one final review? Difficulty at any point in reproducing the following outline indicates areas in which you probably need to review.

I. One _____ (which is a _____

_____.)

II. Two _____ to _____
_____

   A. Rule 1—Use the right _____ for _____ the Bible

      1. Understand the writer's _____

      2. Observe the _____

      3. Accept the _____ of _____

      4. Identify the _____ of _____

      5. Use the Bible to _____ itself

   B. Use correct _____ for _____ the Bible

      1. Apply the Bible according to its _____

      2. Use the Bible as a _____ of _____

      3. Use the _____ properly

      4. Use a _____

understanding

      5. Use the Bible _____

III. Three ways to do Bible _____

   A. _____ Bible study

   B. _____ Bible study

   C. _____ _____ study

IV. Four areas to _____ Bible study

   A. Your own _____

   B. Your relationship with _____

   C. Your relationship with _____

   D. The _____

V. Five aids to _____ Bible study

   A. Understanding _____

   B. Understanding _____ _____

   C. Understanding the _____ of the Bible

   D. Understanding _____ in the Bible

   E. Understanding _____ in the Bible

FINAL REVIEW

You have completed eleven weeks of study. This study has been designed to help you develop skills in the study of God's Word that will make your Christian life more meaningful and fruitful. Let us make one more review of the ground we have covered together. By this time you should be able to use the familiar hand symbol to review this course of study. Take a moment to fill in the appropriate words on each finger. After you write in the various divisions of our study on the fingers, take time to think about each major area of the study.

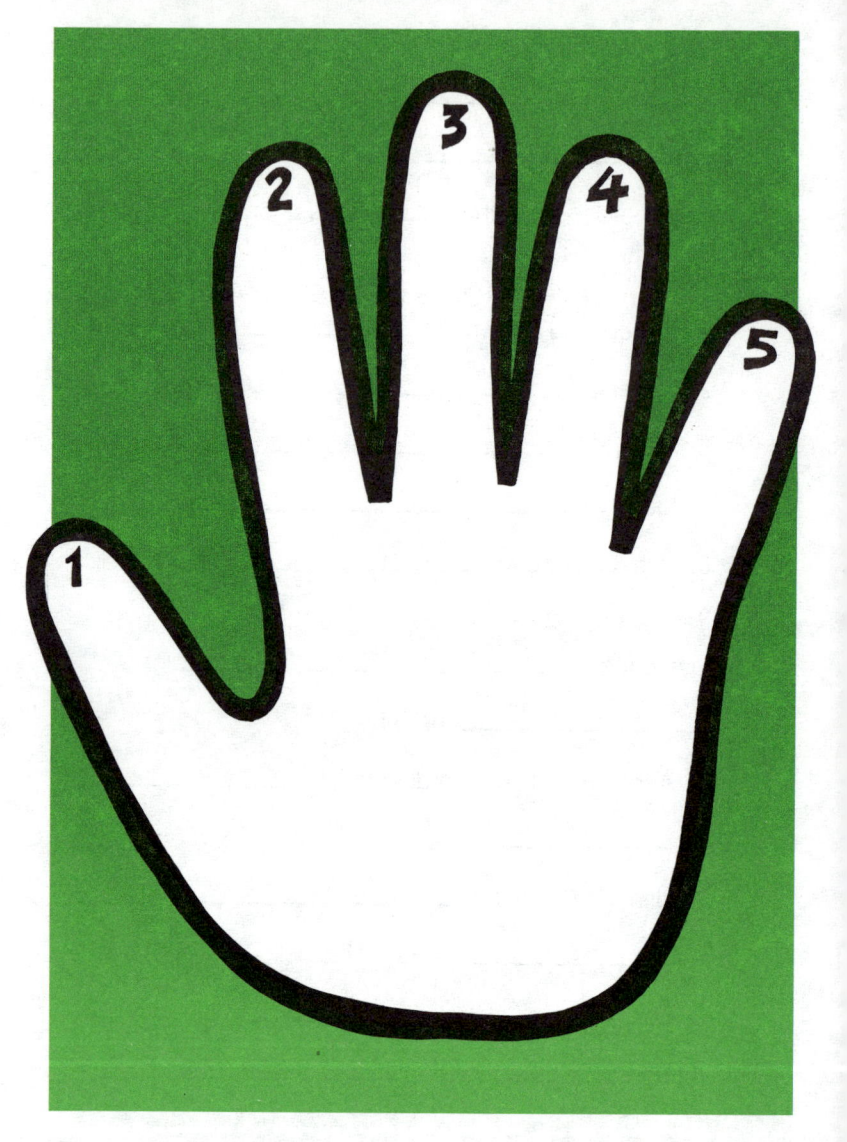

CONCLUSION
WHAT WILL I DO NOW?

You have now finished studying *How to Study Your Bible*. You have learned principles of interpreting and applying the Scripture in your life. You have learned how to master the Bible, apply its teachings wisely, and increase your understanding of its message. Where should you go from here?

You need to practice what you have learned. You started the synthetic method of Bible study with some practice on shorter books such as Philippians and 1 Peter. Choose for yourself a longer book such as Genesis or 1 Corinthians. Practice what you have learned in a synthetic study of these books.

You have learned to use the analytical method of Bible study in a brief passage such as Philippians 4:4-7. Use what you have learned in other passages like this. If you are a Sunday School teacher, study your lessons each week by using the principles of analytical Bible study. If you are teaching fellow students or co-workers in a Bible study, prepare your teaching material by using these principles of Bible study.

You have studied a Bible character such as John Mark. Begin to expand your knowledge of other Bible characters such as Caleb and Joshua in the Old Testament or Barnabas and Mary Magdalene in the New Testament.

Use what you have learned about the study of biblical topics to study additional topics. Use what you have learned about doctrinal Bible study to study the doctrines of salvation, the Holy Spirit, or spiritual gifts. You must be on the lookout for ways in which you can use what you have learned. Practice will make you more skilled.

You also can find help by reading some additional books on interpreting, applying, and studying the Bible. Bernard Ramm has written *Protestant Biblical Interpretation*. If you are interested in learning more about the principles for interpreting and applying the Bible, you should read this book.

Merrill C. Tenney has written *Galatians: the Charter of Christian Liberty*. This helpful Bible study tool uses the Book of Galatians as a laboratory to teach you how to study the Bible using the synthetic approach, the analytical approach, the biographical approach, and the topical approach, plus many others. The book is somewhat advanced over what we have done in *How to Study Your Bible*. Studying this book can take you to a step of higher skill in Bible study.

A helpful book in giving you more information about analytical Bible study is *The Joy of Discovery* by Oletta Wald. The writing is a workbook intended to increase your ability to observe what the Scripture contains and to lead you to interpret it properly.

Another book which covers many of the same methods which we have mentioned in *How to Study Your Bible* is *Twelve Dynamic Bible Study Methods* by Richard Warren. I found much help in using this book as I prepared *How to Study Your Bible*. I am indebted to Richard Warren for many helpful ideas and thoughts which I have included.

Leader's Guide
by Don Atkinson

Welcome to the adventure of studying *How to Study Your Bible* in an adult group. This guide will provide practical suggestions for making this an exciting and profitable study. Before you begin to use this guide, please permit me to make a few suggestions.

- Remember that attending *How to Study Your Bible* in a group is not a substitute for individual study. The group study is built upon the idea of each group member doing the daily work at home.
- In most cases, the group session plan will be built upon some aspect of the individual study from the previous week in *How to Study Your Bible*. There are two exceptions; the first session is introductory and requires no previous work in *How to Study Your Bible* on the part of group members. The final session is designed to give the group members an opportunity to reflect on the entire study and to express their reactions to questions about the study.
- It is vital to the success of the study that you gather resources such as concordances, Bible dictionaries, Bible atlases, and Bible commentaries to use in the sessions. Many of these resources will be found in your church media library. Others can be borrowed from a public library. Your pastor may be willing to let you use some of his books for this study.
- Several sessions call for resource persons to be enlisted. Plan and enlist these persons well in advance. Let them know exactly when you will expect them to visit your group and how much time they will have. Be certain that they will have the materials they need.
- You will need to work faithfully through *How to Study Your Bible* if you are to lead this study.
- Emphasize commitment to the study and covenant with the group. This study will require time and effort.
- As the group leader, you should feel a sense of mission concerning this study. Some members of the group will begin a lifetime of Bible study as a result of this experience. Remember, some group members will be using Bible study tools for the first time. Be sensitive to group members who may tend to become discouraged. Make yourself available to them throughout the study. Your help and encouragement can keep them involved in the group.

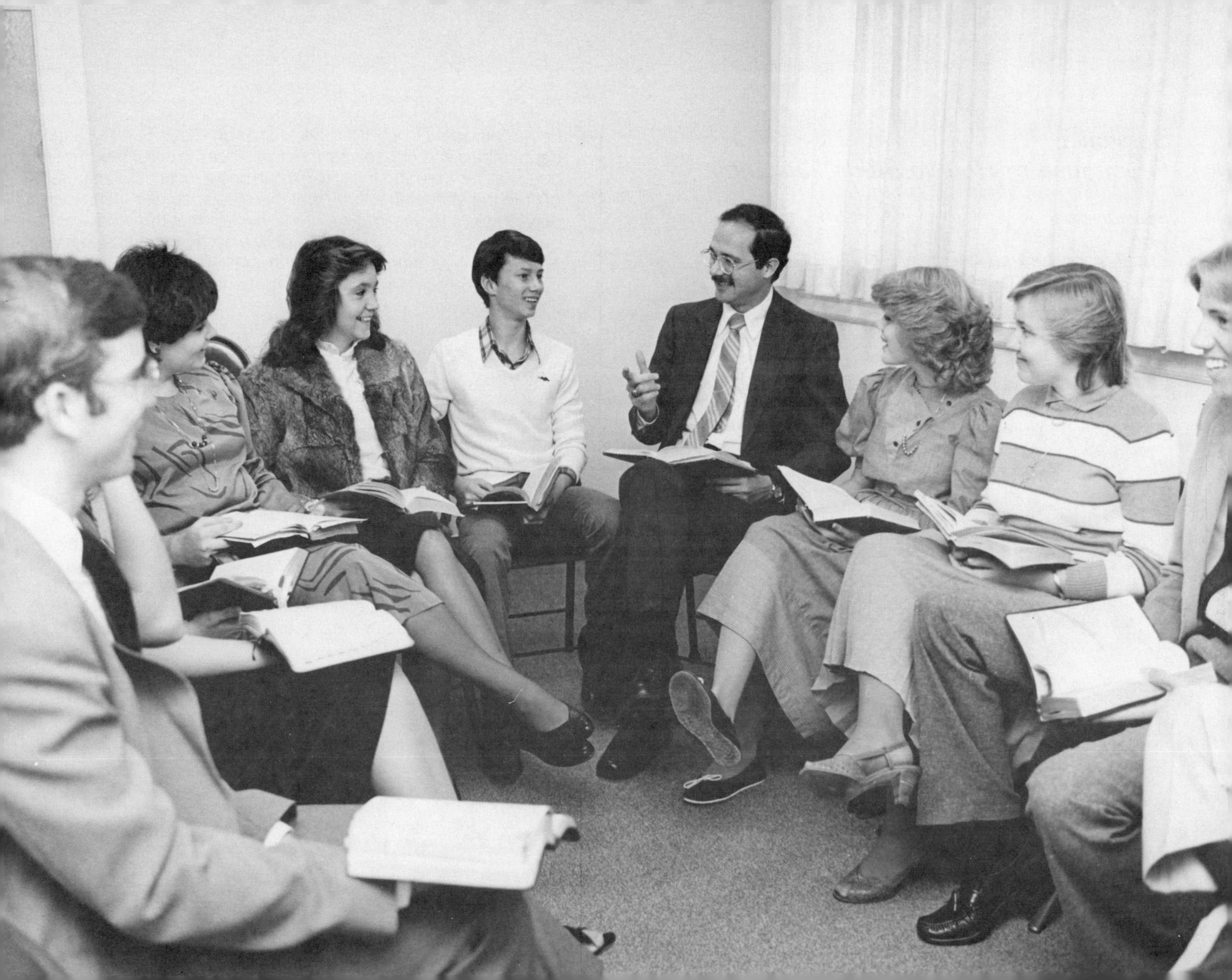

Session 1
Orientation to *How to Study Your Bible*

Session goal: As a result of this session, group members will have—
- been introduced to *How to Study Your Bible;*
- been introduced to the basic tools to be used in this study;
- made a commitment to personal and group study of *How to Study Your Bible.*

Preparing to Lead the Session
- Order a copy of *How to Study Your Bible* for each group member.
- Prepare a commitment/covenant sheet with this statement written at the top, "I commit myself to do the daily work necessary to complete *How to Study Your Bible,* and I covenant to meet with the study group weekly for mutual encouragement and instruction."
- Gather the following Bible study tools for use in the sessions: several translations of the Bible, the Holman *Master Study Bible, The Broadman Bible Commentary,* Bible dictionaries, concordances, and Bible atlases. These can be borrowed from the church media library. Arrange to use these resources for the entire study. Make arrangements for group members to check out these resources.
- Enlist participants prior to the first session. Adult Sunday School departments and classes are the best places to enlist group members. Ask for the opportunity to explain on two successive Sundays prior to the start of the study that this study can help participants develop skills to use in Bible study. Explain that this study will require the commitment to do the daily work in *How to Study Your Bible* as well as participation in the weekly group meetings. Ask that those who want to participate in the study sign the commitment/covenant sheet.
- Provide a meeting room with tables and chairs. Gather materials such as chalkboard, newsprint, colored markers, and masking tape.
- Draw or reproduce the hand emblem found in *How to Study Your Bible* on page 9 for display in the room. An overhead cel of the hand emblem can be used.
- Cover part of a wall in the room with newsprint or tear sheets.
- Become familiar with the contents of *How to Study Your Bible.*

Leading the Session
- As participants arrive, instruct them to go to the wall with the newsprint on it. Ask each person to use a marker to write his or her name and to put a word or symbol beneath the name that describes that person's need to learn how to study the Bible. Take a few minutes to let each person explain what he or she wrote or drew.
- Distribute copies of *How to Study Your Bible* to group members.

- Give a brief overview of *How to Study Your Bible* using the hand diagram. Explain that this course will require each group member to do the daily required work on his or her own. Demonstrate how the memory verses are to be removed from the book and used. Explain that the weekly group meetings will be for the purpose of reviewing, answering questions, and sharing experiences from the previous week's work.
- Call attention to the display of Bible study aids on the table. Tell the group that these resources will be available for use in the group sessions and available to be checked out by group members. Suggest that participants may want to consider purchasing some of these books.
- Ask those who have not done so already to sign the commitment/covenant sheet.
- Divide the group into pairs. Explain that these persons will be encouragers for each other throughout the study. Ask the partners to dialogue for ten minutes using the following questions.
  (1) What brought each of us to this study?
  (2) What personal goal do each of us hope to accomplish through this study?
  (3) How can we assist each other with this study?
  (4) What weekly contract can we make to encourage each other?
- Reassemble the group. Remind them of their commitment to do the daily study and their covenant with the group. Close the session with prayer.

Session 2
One Prerequisite for Bible Study

Session goal: As a result of this session, group members will be able to demonstrate an understanding of how spiritual hunger serves as a prerequisite to Bible study by—
- identifying the five aspects of spiritual hunger;
- explaining why each aspect is vital in studying the Bible.

Preparing to Lead the Session
- Do the daily work in week 1 of *How to Study Your Bible*.
- Provide materials such as newsprint, crayons, marking pens, construction paper, foil, poster board, modeling clay, and paper for use in this session.
- Enlist someone who is a good Bible student to give a five-minute testimony on the topic "How Bible Study Satisfies My Spiritual Needs."

Leading the Session
- Welcome those present. Have someone sing or read a verse of the hymn "Holy Bible, Book Divine." Ask for prayer requests concerning any needs in the group. Call on a group member to lead in prayer.
- Take five minutes to answer any questions that have arisen concerning the individual study in *How to Study Your Bible*.
- Divide the group into five smaller groups. This can be five pairs, or even five individuals, according to the size of the group. Assign one of the five aspects of the spiritual hunger study to each group. They are as follows.
  (1) Being a Christian
  (2) Eagerness to learn
  (3) Teachable attitude
  (4) Dependence on the Holy Spirit
  (5) Discipline
  Ask the small groups to consider why the topic they are considering is vital to Bible study. Ask each group to draw, write, or make something out of the materials available that will demonstrate its topic. Reassemble the larger group and let each group report. Allow twenty-five minutes for this activity.
- Ask the person enlisted to give a five-minute testimony on how Bible study satisfies spiritual needs.
- If time permits, allow group members to react to the testimony by asking any questions they wish to ask.
- Close the session by having the group join hands to pray for spiritual hunger for Bible study.

Session 3
Rules to Guide Bible Study

Session goal: As a result of this session, group members will be able to demonstrate an understanding of the guidelines for Bible study found in week 2 of *How to Study Your Bible* by—
- explaining the meaning of each guideline;
- using assigned passages from the Bible to illustrate these guidelines.

Preparing to Lead the Session
- Work through week 2 in *How to Study Your Bible*.
- Prepare a poster with the heading "Guidelines for Interpreting the Bible." List from top to bottom the following guidelines.
  (1) Literal meaning
  (2) Context
  (3) Limits of revelation
  (4) Type of writing
  (5) Bible as interpreter
  Cover each entry on the list with a strip of paper. Attach the strips with masking tape.
- Have several Bible commentaries available for use in the session.
- Prepare five assignment cards as follows:
  The Literal Meaning
  1. Read 1 Corinthians 16:1-4 and Isaiah 55:12-13.
  2. What do you think the writers literally meant? Does one passage seem more literal than the other?
  3. Are there words or phrases in either of these passages that cannot be taken in a literal sense?

Understanding the Context
1. Read Matthew 6:3.
2. Could someone misuse this one verse to prove that a person should not make a stewardship pledge or allow the church to keep a record of giving?
3. Read Matthew 6:1-4. This puts verse 3 in context. What does verse 3 mean in its context?

Limits of Revelation
1. Read 2 Timothy 3:14-17.
2. What does this passage teach about the specific purpose of Scripture?
3. Are there any areas of human knowledge that may not be dealt with in the teachings of the Bible?

Type of Writing
1. Locate a passage in the Bible that fits each of the following categories: narrative (the record of an event), parable, poetry, prophecy, and a letter.

The Bible as Interpreter
1. Read John 6:52-58. In this passage, Jesus spoke of believers eating His flesh and drinking His blood. Some people have found this passage puzzling. How would reading the entire chapter help in understanding what Jesus meant by eating His flesh and drinking His blood?
2. Read Exodus 16. How could this passage help a person understand John 6?
3. Read Mark 14:22-24. This passage describes the meaning of the Lord's Supper. How could this passage help a person understand John 6:52-58?

Leading the Session
- Welcome all group members.
- Review the memory verses.
- Take a few minutes to share experiences on difficulties from the past week's study of *How to Study Your Bible*. If you sense that any individual is having difficulty keeping up with the group, plan a contact with that person this week.
- Present a ten-minute review lecture covering the five guidelines. Use the covered poster. Uncover each guideline as you discuss it.
- Divide the group into five smaller groups. If the total group is small,

use five pairs. If necessary, use five individuals rather than groups. Assign each group one of the five assignment cards. Instruct the groups to discuss their assignments. Suggest that they use the commentaries that are on display when appropriate. Make yourself available to help the groups as needed. Allow about fifteen minutes for this group work.
- Reassemble the group. Have each smaller group report on its assignment.
- Close the session by reminding the group of their commitment/covenant. Ask whether each person is meeting with his or her partner on a regular basis. Lead the group in prayer.

Session 4
Correct Principles for Applying the Bible

Session goal: As a result of this session, group members will be able to demonstrate an understanding of the principles for applying the Bible by—
- writing a brief definition of each principle;
- classifying selected Bible promises as universal, limited, personal, or conditional.

Preparing to Lead the Session
- Work through week 3 of *How to Study Your Bible*.
- Enlist the pastor or some other person who is knowledgeable concerning Bible study to give a fifteen-minute lecture on the five principles for applying the Bible found in week 3 of *How to Study Your Bible*.
- Prepare a listening sheet for group members. The heading on this sheet should be "Principles for Applying the Bible." List five principles on the sheet as follows: (1) apply according to its real meaning; (2) use as a book of principles; (3) use the promises properly; (4) use a cross-cultural understanding; (5) use wisely.
Leave several lines between each for writing.
- Secure four pouch-type file folders. On the outside of each folder, print one of the following with a marker: Universal, Limited, Personal, Conditional. These should be attached to a bulletin board with thumbtacks or on the wall with masking tape. Be sure that the folder pouch is left open.
- Prepare slips of paper with the following promise references written on them: John 1:12; John 6:47; John 5:24; 2 Corinthians 5:1; Isaiah

26:3; Proverbs 3:5-6; Matthew 6:14; Malachi 3:10; Proverbs 3:9-10; Philippians 1:6; Proverbs 22:6; James 5:16; Acts 1:8; John 16:13; Psalm 33:18; John 16:24; Deuteronomy 11:26-28; Philippians 4:7; Luke 11:9; John 14:13-14; John 15:7; Jeremiah 29:13; Micah 7:7; 2 Corinthians 12:9; Psalm 28:7; Psalm 46:1; Philippians 4:13; Philippians 4:19; James 4:6.

Leading the Session
- Open the session with prayer.
- Review the memory verses for week 3 of *How to Study Your Bible*.
- Introduce the pastor or other resource person you have enlisted to give the lecture on principles for applying the Bible. The lecture should last no more than fifteen minutes.
- Distribute the prepared listening sheets. Instruct group members to listen to the guest lecturer and write a definition of each of the five principles.
- Give out slips of paper with the Bible references written on them. Ask each person to look up his verse or verses. When everyone has had time to read the verses silently, have the verses read aloud. They are all promises found in the Bible. Ask each person to place the reference in the file folder pouch that represents the type of promise it is. As time permits, allow the group to react by saying whether they agree with the way each promise is classified. If there is disagreement, let the group decide in which category the promise in question belongs.
- Close the session with prayer.

Session 5
Synthetic Bible Study

Session goal: As a result of this session, group members will be able to demonstrate an understanding of synthetic Bible study by—
- participating in a discussion of synthetic Bible study;
- using the Book Summary Chart in a small group.

Preparing to Lead the Session
- Work through the material in week 4 of *How to Study Your Bible*. Give special attention to the Paragraph Summary Form and the Book Summary Chart.
- Provide Bibles in several translations for use in the session.
- Draw the charts found on page 45 and 46 of *How to Study Your Bible* on large sheets of newsprint. Use overhead cels if you prefer.

Leading the Session
- Welcome all group members.
- Review the memory verses for the week.
- Take a few minutes to discuss any questions, problems, or difficulties group members have encountered in the past week of study.
- Review the meaning of synthetic Bible study. Explain that it refers to a type of study that looks at a book of the Bible as a whole. As you define it, let group members ask questions and make comments concerning this method of Bible study.
- From your own study notes for the week, demonstrate the use of the Paragraph Summary Form on the large newsprint or on the overhead cel.
- From your own study notes for the week, demonstrate the use of the Book Summary Chart on the large newsprint or on the overhead cel. Try to make certain that all group members understand the use of these charts.
- Divide the group into three smaller groups. Explain that the groups will use the Book Summary Chart for the next activity. Assign one of the Bible books studied in week 4 of *How to Study Your Bible* to each group. Instruct groups to share their week's study of the book. Ask them to report on the first chapter or major division. Suggest that the groups report the title or theme they gave to the first chapter or major division. Ask that they conclude their report by giving a summary of the key ideas of the paragraphs in the first chapter or major division of the book of the Bible they have studied in their group.
- Close with prayer.

Session 6
Analytical Bible Study

Session goal: As a result of this session, group members will be able to demonstrate an understanding of analytical Bible study by—
- identifying the five ways to do analytical Bible study and placing them on the analytical Bible study chart;
- doing either a paraphrase or a summary of a passage from the Bible.

Preparing to Lead the Session
- Arrange to have several modern translations of the Bible available for use in the session.
- Reproduce the arch from page 52 in *How to Study Your Bible* on a large poster. Leave the five sections of the arch blank. Provide marking pens.
- Prior to the session, enlist five group members to give a brief explanation of the following: "Make a paraphrase"; "Use observations, questions and answers"; "Apply the Bible"; "Make a comparison"; "Summarize the content." Limit these presentations to three minutes each.
- Provide paper and pencils for writing.

Leading the Session
- Open the session with prayer.
- Give participants an opportunity to share experiences related to the past week of study.
- Review the memory verses for week 5.
- Call on group members who were enlisted to make the three-minute presentations. As each person makes the assigned pre-

sentation, have someone use a marker to fill in the appropriate section of the arch. Take time after each presentation to make certain that all group members understand each point.
- Ask each member of the group to choose one of the following activities.
  (1) Write a paraphrase of Colossians 1:15-18. This should be done without using a modern language translation. After the paraphrase is written, a modern language translation can be checked.
  (2) Write a summary of the contents of Colossians 1:15-18. Use modern language translations to help you write this summary. Provide paper and pencils for this activity.
- After the paraphrases and summaries are written, divide both the paraphrasers and the summarizers into pairs. Take five minutes for the pairs to share their work with each other.
- Encourage partners to meet this week for mutual help and encouragement.
- Close the session with prayer for guidance in the weeks of study ahead.

Session 7
Background Bible Study

Session goal: As a result of this session, group members will be able to demonstrate an understanding of background Bible study by—
- being able to explain why background study is important in Bible study;
- practicing using Bible study tools that provide background information.

Preparing to Lead the Session
- Prepare a brief lecture on the importance of background Bible study.
- Gather the following Bible study aids for display and use in this session: concordances, reference Bibles, Bible dictionaries, Bible atlases, and Bible commentaries.
- Set up four tables or work areas in the room. If possible, use adjoining or nearby rooms for two of the work areas.
- Make strips from adding-machine tape that designate the work areas as follows: (1) using a concordance, (2) using a Bible dictionary, (3) using a Bible atlas, (4) using a Bible commentary.

- Enlist four capable Bible students in your church to lead five-to-eight-minute studies on the use of Bible study tools. Assign one person the responsibility to lead a study on how to use the Bible concordance, another the responsibility to lead a study on how to use a Bible dictionary, another on how to use a Bible atlas, and the fourth person on how to use a Bible commentary. Contact these leaders well in advance of the session and ask them to prepare to give instructions and a practical demonstration of the Bible study tool they are assigned. Explain that each of them will make the presentation four times. Provide paper, pencils, newsprint, markers, and any other supplies that these persons need.

Leading the Session
- Welcome all group members. Have a time of prayer.
- Review the memory work from week 6 of *How to Study Your Bible*.
- Give a brief lecture (5 minutes) on the importance of background Bible study.
- Tell the group that this session will focus on using Bible study tools for background Bible study. Explain that four learning centers have been set up to help them learn or review the use of some tools for Bible study. Explain that each person will go to each learning center, then move on to the next center until all four centers have been visited.
- Divide the group into four smaller groups. Number the groups 1 through 4. Ask group 1 to begin at the learning center where the concordance will be studied. Ask group 2 to go to the table where the study will be on using the Bible dictionary. Ask group 3 to go to the table where the Bible atlas will be studied. Ask group 4 to go to the table where using a Bible commentary will be studied.
- After eight minutes, give a signal to instruct the groups to rotate to the next table. Continue the process until each of the four groups have been to each of the four tables.
- Reassemble the group for closing comments. If time permits, ask group members to share their experiences from tonight's session. Ask whether they feel that this method of using learning stations has been helpful.
- Close with prayer. Give special prayer attention to needs that have been expressed by group members.

Session 8
How to Do and Apply a Biographical Study

Session goal: As a result of this session, group members will be able to demonstrate an understanding of four areas to apply Bible study by—
- sharing with another person the work done on page 77 to apply John 13:34-45;
- completing an assigned biographical study during the session.

Preparing to Lead the Session
- Work through week 7 of *How to Study Your Bible*.
- Prepare copies of Biographical Study Worksheet (p. 80 of *How to Study Your Bible*) and How I Can Apply This Study (p. 83 of *How to Study Your Bible*). Prepare one for each member on 8½ by 11 paper. Have additional paper available. Provide pencils.
- Prepare poster or overhead cel with the heading "Four Areas to Apply Bible Study." List the four areas as follows: (1) our relationship with God, (2) our relationship with others, (3) to ourselves, and (4) to the church.
- Feature several Bible concordances, Bible dictionaries, Bible encyclopedias, and commentaries on the Book of Acts for use in this session.

Leading the Session
- Welcome group members. Have a time of sharing concerns and prayer.
- Review memory work for the past week of study.
- Present a brief review of the four ways to apply Bible study using the poster or cel that was prepared.
- Divide the group into pairs. Ask members to share with their partner the work they did on applying John 13:34-45 (p. 77).
- Reassemble the group. Distribute the two worksheets you prepared for this session. Ask each person to use these worksheets to do a character study on Philip, the evangelist. Explain that the story of Philip is found in the Book of Acts. Remind group members that concordances, Bible dictionaries, Bible encyclopedias, and commentaries on Acts are available in the room. Also, instruct them to use the Biographical Study Worksheet and the How I Can Apply This Study worksheet. Each person will work on his or her own character study. Group members will share the study resources.
- If time permits, allow ten minutes for group members to share their study with the group.
- Close with prayer.

Session 9
Character Trait and Devotional Bible Study

Session goal: As a result of this session, group members will be able to demonstrate an understanding of character trait Bible study and devotional Bible study by—
- listing the eight steps for doing a character trait Bible study;
- doing a character trait Bible study with a partner;
- participating in a devotional Bible study with the group.

Preparing to Lead the Session
- Work through week 8 of *How to Study Your Bible*.
- Provide paper and pencils for group members.
- Prepare Character Trait Bible Study worksheet using the one on page 86 of *How to Study Your Bible* as your model.
- Use a large sheet of newsprint to make a replica of the Devotional Bible Study worksheet on page 91 of *How to Study Your Bible*. Place another sheet beside the worksheet. Use the heading on that sheet "Ways This Passage Can Be Applied." Then, list the following, leaving room to write beneath each one: (1) to your relationship with God, (2) to your own life, (3) to your relationship with others, and (4) to the church. Use two sheets of newsprint for this, if necessary.

- Have a collection of concordances, topical Bibles, and Bible dictionaries on hand for use in this session.

Leading the Session
- Welcome all group members. Ask whether members have special prayer requests and call on someone to lead in prayer. Review the memory work for the past week. Emphasize the importance of doing the memory work. Take a few minutes to answer questions concerning week 8 of *How to Study Your Bible*. If you sense that any group member is having problems with the study or is becoming discouraged, plan a personal contact with that person.
- Ask group members to list the eight steps for doing a character trait Bible study (pp. 86-87). Ask them to make this list without referring to the book. Allow five minutes for this activity. Review these steps and ask group members to fill in those they were unable to list.
- Ask each person to meet with his/her partner to do a fifteen-minute character trait Bible study. Instruct the pairs to work together on the character trait of loyalty. Ask them to draw upon their experience in the past week as they have studied *How to Study Your Bible*. Ask that they record their findings on the Character Trait Bible Study worksheet. Each pair will need a topical Bible, a concordance, or a Bible dictionary to use in the study.
- Reassemble the group. Allow ten minutes for sharing this exercise. Let the sharing time be general, rather than having each group report.
- Lead the group in a devotional Bible study of 1 Corinthians 12 in the following way.

(1) Ask each group member to read the passage and think about it for a moment.
(2) Use the outline of the Devotional Bible Study worksheet you have on the wall to lead the group through the study. Do the study by group participation. Ask the group to work together to complete the large sheet with the heading Ways This Passage Can Be Applied.

- Ask for brief comments from the groups concerning how the work with their study partners is going. Encourage partners to plan a time together each week. Ask group members to bring their completed word study worksheets to next week's group session and to be prepared to share.
- Close with prayer.

Session 10
How to Do a Word Study

Session goal: As a result of this session, group members will be able to demonstrate an understanding of week 9 of *How to Study Your Bible* by—
- listing the four guidelines for a Bible word study;
- sharing their word study notes from the past week with the group.

Preparing to Lead the Session
- Work through week 9 of *How to Study Your Bible*.
- Use four sheets of newsprint or poster board and markers to make four posters from the guidelines given on pages 96 and 97 of *How to Study Your Bible*. Make a summary statement of one or two sentences for each of these. Plan a way to conceal these posters

until you are ready to use them. If you use newsprint, you can simply fold the bottom of the poster up and attach it to the top with pieces of masking tape. Remove the tape and let the posters drop down when you are ready to use them, one at a time.
- Prepare a five-minute lecture on the four guidelines.
- Provide paper and pencils for use in the session.
- Use a chalkboard, newsprint, or an overhead cel to reproduce the Word Study Worksheet on page 97.

Leading the Session
- Welcome all group members.
- Open the session with a time of sharing and prayer.
- Review memory verses from the past week of study.
- Present a five-minute lecture on the four guidelines for doing a word study. Display each guideline poster as you explain that guideline. Fold or cover the poster when you are finished with the explanation.
- Distribute paper and pencils to group members. Ask them to list the four guidelines for a word study. When everyone is finished, uncover the posters once again as group members check their answers.
- Guide the group through a sharing of their word study notes from last week's *How to Study Your Bible* study. Use the poster, chalkboard, or overhead cel of the Word Study Worksheet to guide the sharing. Let this be a time of general sharing. Try to involve all members of the group in this activity.
- Close the session with prayer.

Session 11
Understanding Biblical Images

Session goal: As a result of this session, group members will be able to demonstrate an understanding of biblical images by—
- participating in a discussion concerning figures of speech in the Bible;
- locating various figures of speech in selected Bible passages.

Preparing to Lead the Session
- Work through the material in *How to Study Your Bible* which relates to biblical images. This will include day 4 of week 9 through day 4 of week 10 (pp. 102-113).
- Enlist a person who is knowledgeable in the area of language arts as a resource person. A high school or college instructor in this area would be a good choice. Give this person a copy of *How to Study Your Bible*. Ask the person to study pages 102-113 carefully to prepare to lead a twenty-minute study of the figures of speech mentioned in this section of *How to Study Your Bible*.
- Prepare group assignment cards. The cards should be prepared in this way: place the name of one of the figures of speech at the top of each card. Beneath the title, write "Find examples of this figure of speech in the following passages from the Bible: Metaphor: Luke 12:32; John 10:16; Luke 8:21; Luke 22:31; Isaiah 59:1; Psalm 44:3. Simile: Luke 10:3; Matthew 23:37; Matthew 24:27; Isaiah 1:8; 1 Thessalonians 5:2; Jeremiah 23:29. Synecdoche: Judges 12:7; Micah 4:3; Joel 3:10. Hyperbole: John 21:25; Deuteronomy 1:28; Romans 4:19. Euphemism: Acts 1:24-25; Leviticus 18:6. Metonymy: Genesis 42:38; Romans 3:27-30; Luke 16:29. Personification: Matthew 6:34; Psalm 114:1-8. Rhetorical Question: Romans 4:9-10; Romans 8:31-35."
- Make several King James Version Bibles available for group members to use.

Leading the Session
- Welcome all group members. Share prayer concerns. Review memory work.
- Introduce the resource person enlisted to lead a twenty-minute study on figures of speech. Explain that the purpose of this study is to make certain that group members understand the figures of speech and their importance in Bible study. Tell the group that they are invited to ask the resource person questions concerning any of the figures of speech.
- Ask group members to pair up with the partner with whom they have worked throughout this study. Give each pair an assignment card to discover figures of speech in passages from the Bible. If you have more pairs than cards, make duplicate assignments. If you have fewer pairs than cards, choose assignments from the cards. Ask the pairs to find their assigned figures of speech in the Bible passages on their cards. Instruct group members to read these passages from the King James Version. Allow fifteen minutes for this work.
- Reassemble the group and hear as many reports as possible in the remaining time.
- Announce that the next session will be the final one in the study of *How to Study Your Bible*. Tell the group to come to the next session prepared to answer some questions designed to evaluate the study.
- Announce that there will be a time of fellowship and refreshments at the next session. Ask for any help you need in providing for refreshments.
- Close the session with prayer.

Session 12
Conclusion

Session goal: As a result of this session, group members will be able to evaluate their eleven-week study in *How to Study Your Bible* by—
- responding to evaluative questions in a circle response activity;
- making a commitment to personal Bible study as a life discipline.

Preparing to Lead the Session
This session will focus on giving group members the opportunity to evaluate the study experience they have had over the past weeks as they have studied *How to Study Your Bible*. In this sense it will differ from the other sessions that have focused on some particular part of *How to Study Your Bible*.
- Remove tables and displays from the room. Arrange chairs in a circle.
- Prepare questions for a circle response activity. A circle response activity is conducted by having all group members seated in a circle. The leader asks questions, and each person in the circle makes a response. No group member may speak twice until everyone has responded to the question. After everyone has spoken, any group member may speak again before the next question is asked. The process continues until all questions are asked. The following questions are suggested. Add others if you wish.
    (1) Why do you think Bible study is important for Christians?
    (2) Do you feel that your study of *How to Study Your Bible* has been helpful in your Bible study?
    (3) Can you recall one new thing you have learned in this study?
    (4) What part of the study did you find most interesting?
    (5) What part of the study did you find least helpful?
    (6) Of the various types of Bible study we have used in our study, which did you like best?

(7) Which did you enjoy most, the personal study of *How to Study Your Bible* or the group activities?
(8) What did you enjoy most about the group meetings?
(9) What did you enjoy least about the group meetings?
(10) What would you suggest to make the group meetings more interesting?
(11) What is your reaction to having worked with a partner during this study?
(12) What are your personal plans to continue your commitment to Bible study?

- If possible, plan to have group members recognized in a worship service of the church.
- Plan light refreshments for a time of fellowship.

Leading the Session

- As group members arrive, ask them to be seated in the circle.
- Give group members the opportunity to share prayer concerns. Pray together, allowing anyone around the circle who wishes to do so to lead in prayer.
- Explain that this session is not related specifically to the final week of *How to Study Your Bible*. Instead, this session will be a time of sharing experiences and insights from the entire study. Explain that they are seated in a circle in order to have a circle response activity. Tell them that you will ask several questions and give them the opportunity to respond. Explain that no person should make a second response until everyone who wishes to do so has responded. Ask that each person make a response to each question. Proceed with the circle response activity.
- If you have arranged for group members to be recognized in a worship service, share these plans with the group.
- Save at least fifteen minutes at the close of the session for refreshments and fellowship.
- Ask the group members to join hands for a closing prayer.

CHRISTIAN GROWTH STUDY PLAN

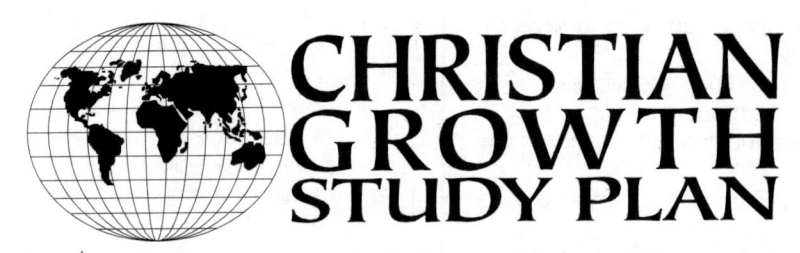

Preparing Christians to Serve

In the **Christian Growth Study Plan (formerly Church Study Course), How to Study Your Bible** is a resource for course credit in the subject area Bible Studies of the Christian Growth category of diploma plans. To receive credit, read the book, complete the learning activities, show your work to your pastor, a staff member or church leader, then complete the following information. This page may be duplicated. Send the completed page to:

Christian Growth Study Plan
127 Ninth Avenue, North, MSN 117
Nashville, TN 37234-0117
FAX: (615) 251-5067

For information about the Christian Growth Study Plan, refer to the current Christian Growth Study Plan Catalog. Your church office may have a copy. If not, request a free copy from the Christian Growth Study Plan office (615/251-2525).

How to Study Your Bible
COURSE NUMBER: CG-0102

PARTICIPANT INFORMATION

Social Security Number

Personal CGSP Number*

Date of Birth

Name (First, MI, Last)
- [ ] Mr. [ ] Miss
- [ ] Mrs. [ ]

Home Phone

Address (Street, Route, or P.O. Box)

City, State

Zip Code

CHURCH INFORMATION

Church Name

Address (Street, Route, or P. O. Box)

City, State

Zip Code

CHANGE REQUEST ONLY

- [ ] Former Name
- [ ] Former Address — City, State — Zip Code
- [ ] Former Church — Zip Code

Signature of Pastor, Conference Leader, or Other Church Leader

Date

*New participants are requested but not required to give SS# and date of birth. Existing participants, please give CGSP# when using SS# for the first time. Thereafter, only one ID# is required. Mail to: Christian Growth Study Plan, 127 Ninth Ave., North, MSN 117, Nashville, TN 37234-0117. Fax: (615)251-5067